BLANK COMIC BOOK for Kids

Create Your Own
Comics With This
Comic Book
Journal Notebook

www.blankcomicbooks.com

The awesome creator of this Comic Book is

How to use this book

This blank comic book is filled with fun templates ready for you to create your own unique comic book stories. Let your imagination run wild as you create, draw and color to bring your comics to life.

You will love filling out the different frames and boxes. Some of the comic pages have speech bubbles in place and others are left blank for you to use your own imagination putting your speech bubbles exactly where you want.

Think about the words you will use as well as sound effects, titles, captions, word and thought bubbles. Add interesting text too. Draw your illustrations / pictures and color it all in, your comic will come to life one page at a time.
There is a mixture of blank comic strips and comic strips with speech bubbles so you can mix and match and come up with your own amazing stories.

There's room for you to create lots of comics grouped into double page spreads, different themes and also layouts for you to create fast action one page illustrative stories. These are great when you just want to create a quick comic when your head is buzzing with fresh ideas.

If you enjoy this book, please consider leaving a review for us as this will help others to find and enjoy the book too. So the last thing to say is "what are you waiting for?" Get your pencils out and start creating your very own comic book.

Speech Bubbles & Words

Use your imagination to come up with words to put in your speech bubbles. The illustrations below are an example of some words you could use.

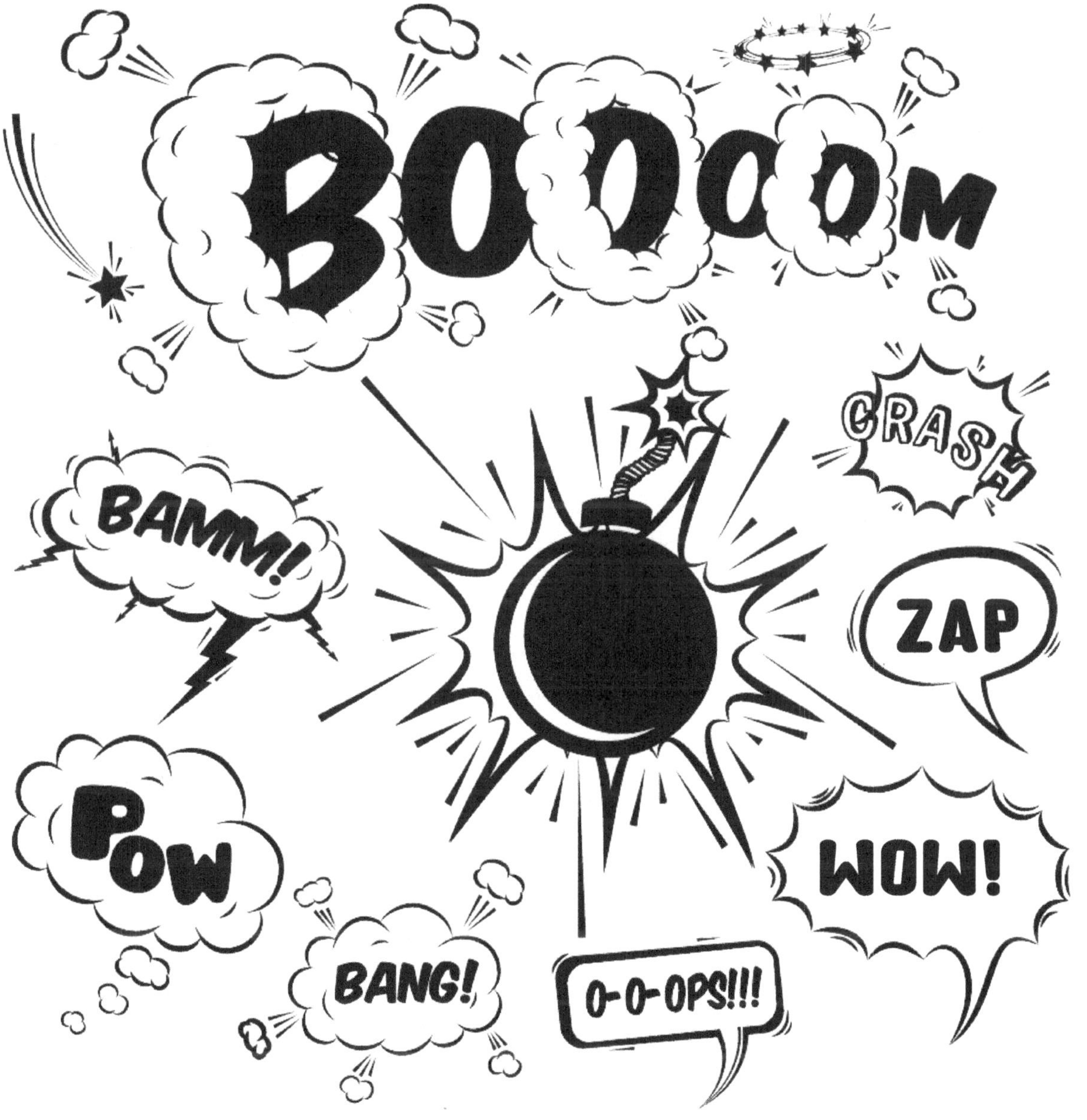

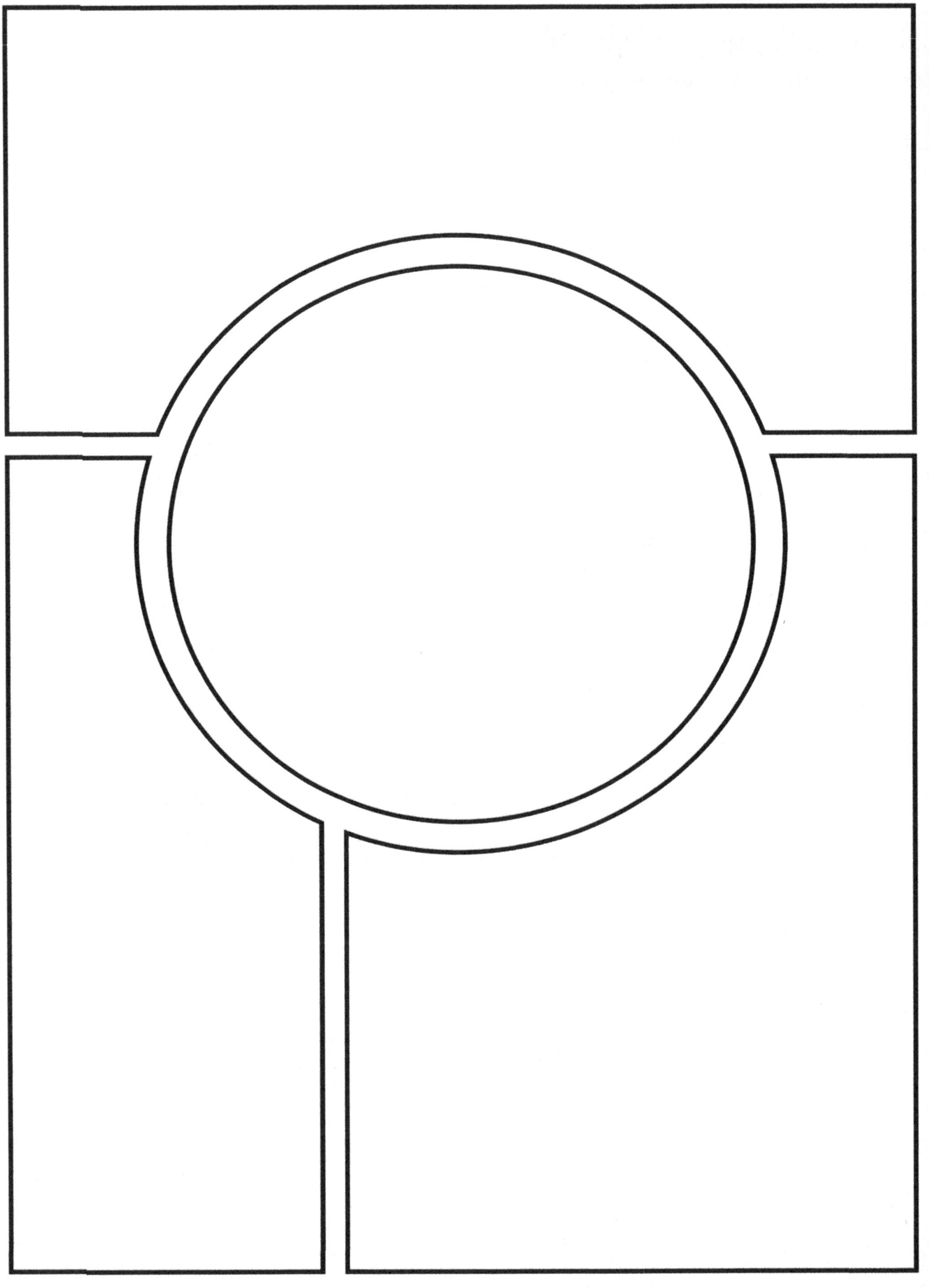

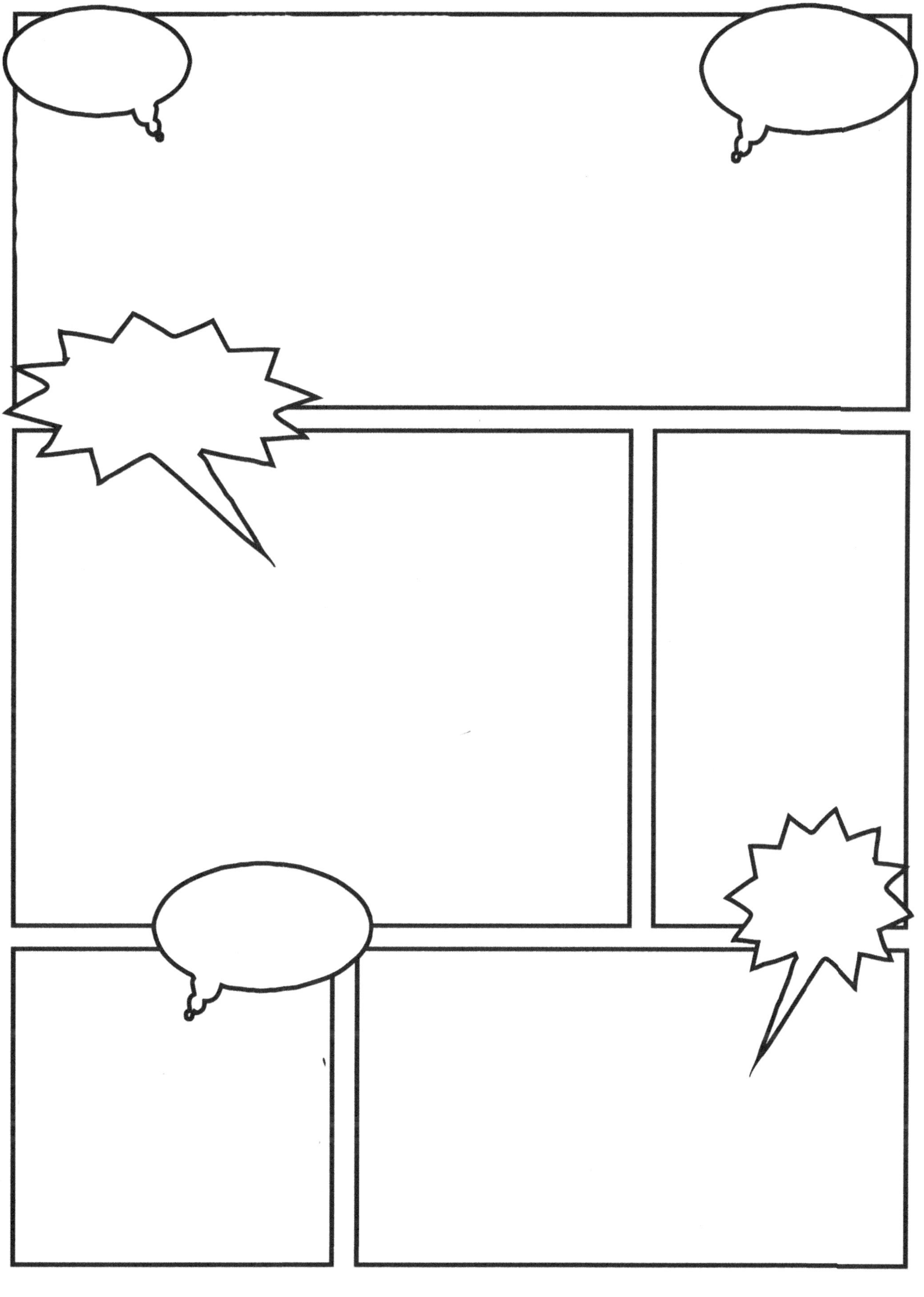

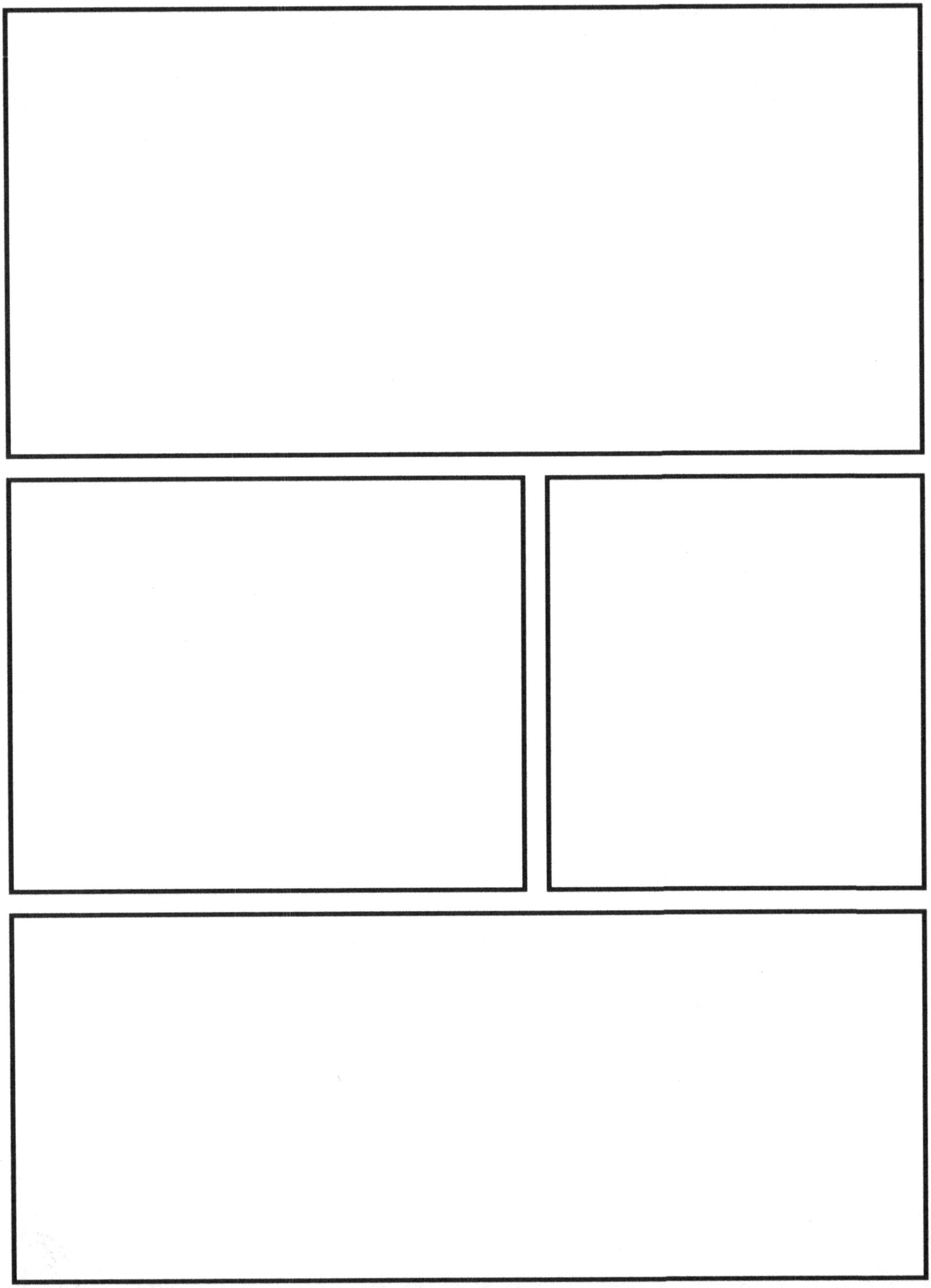

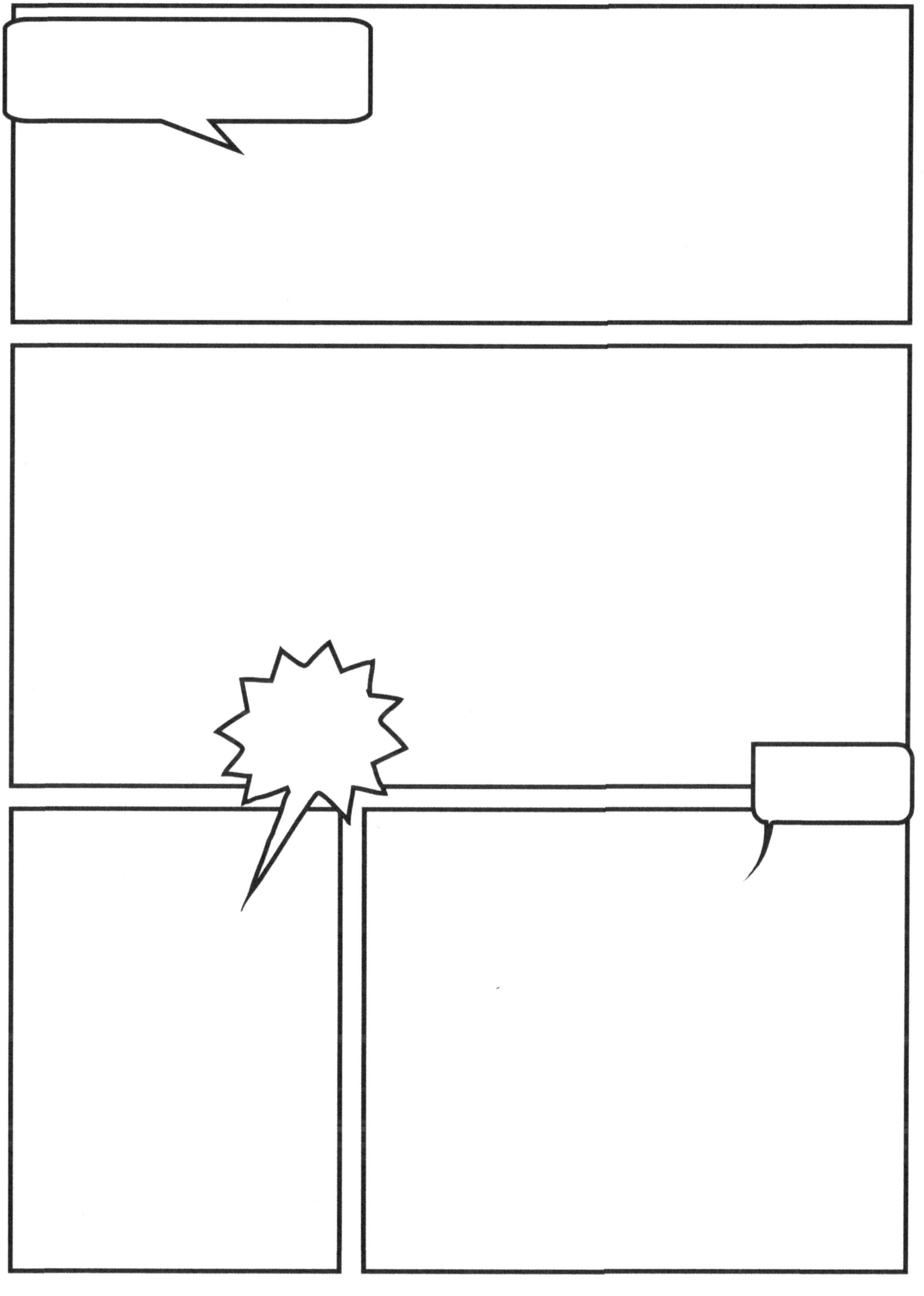

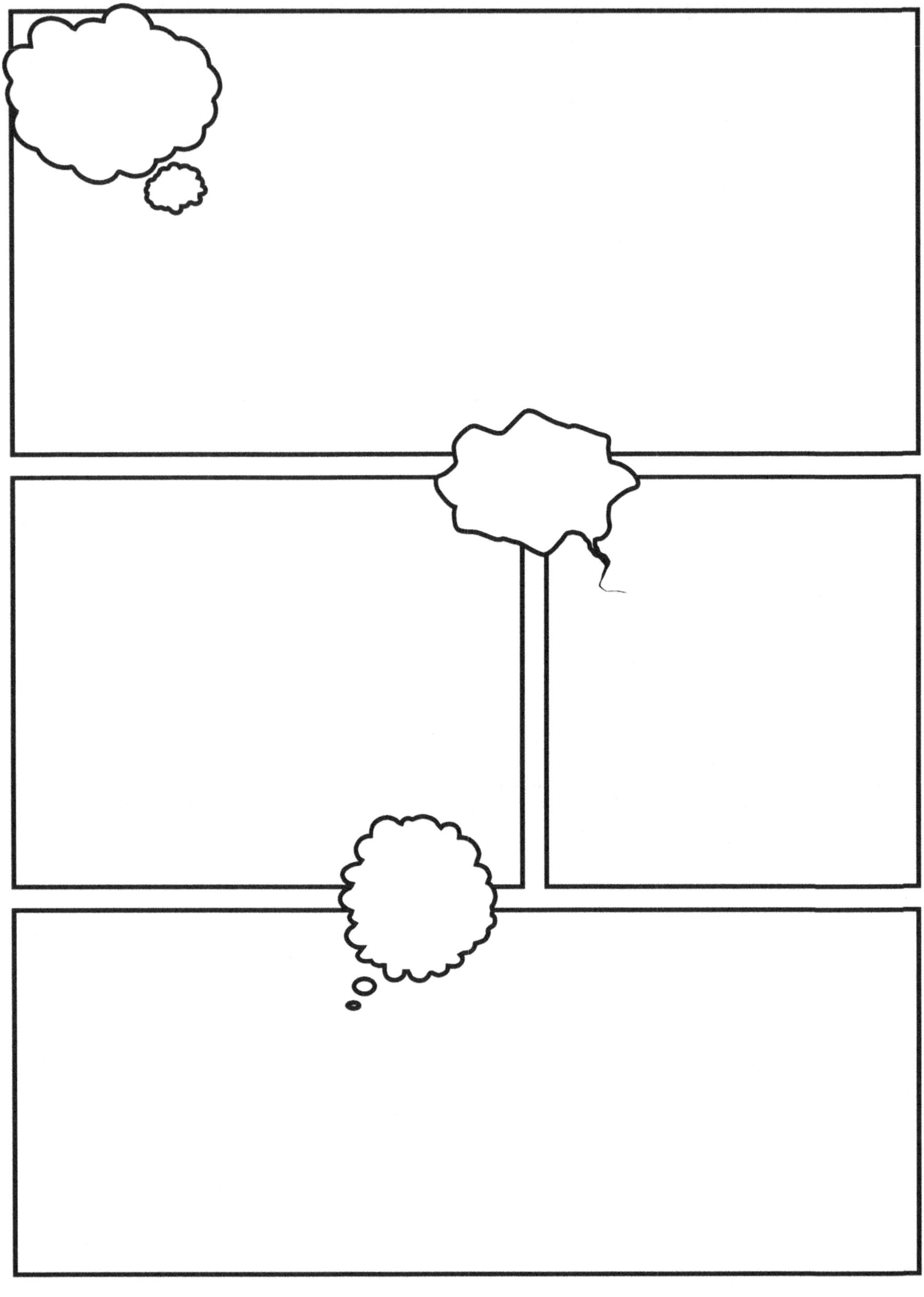

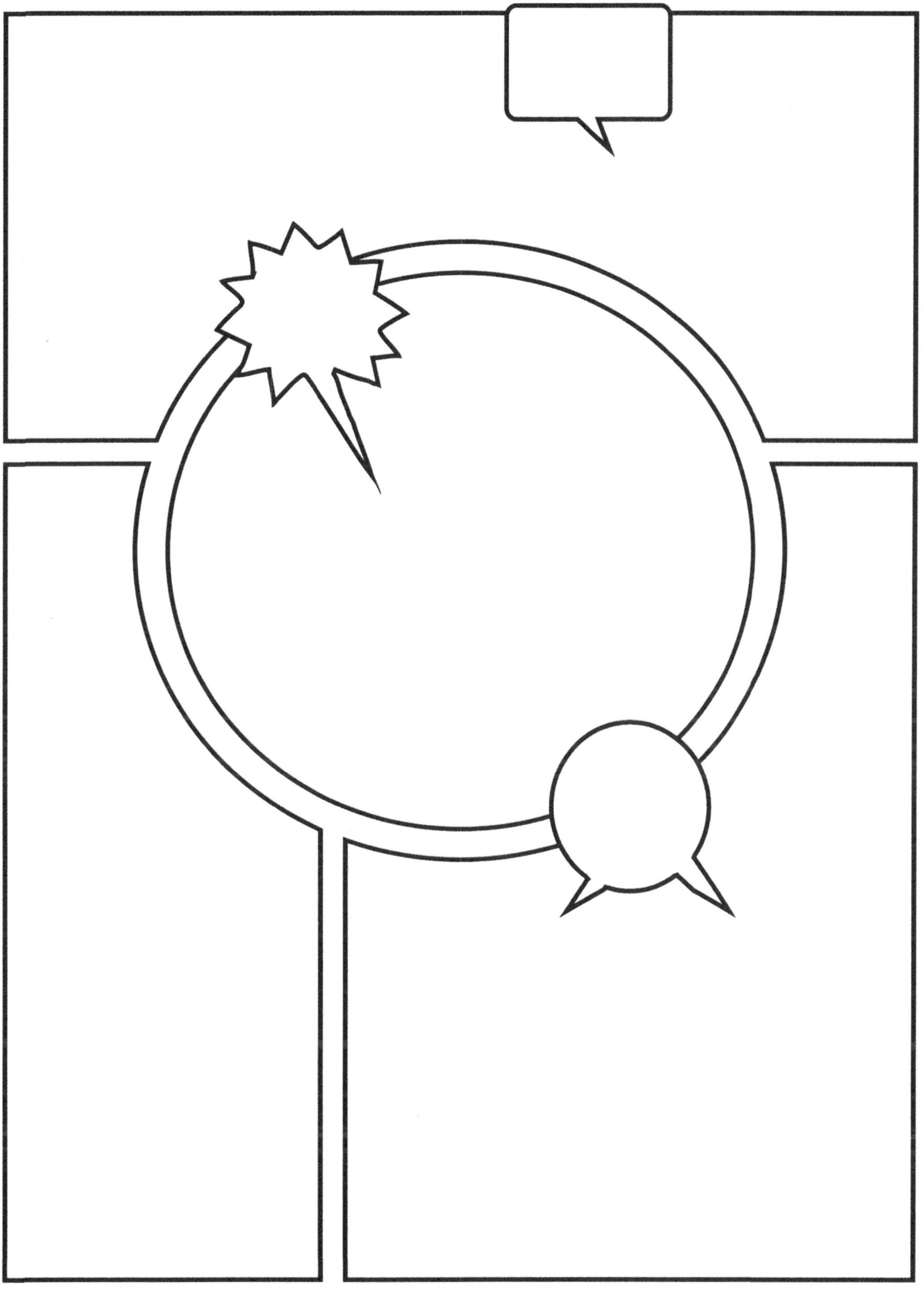

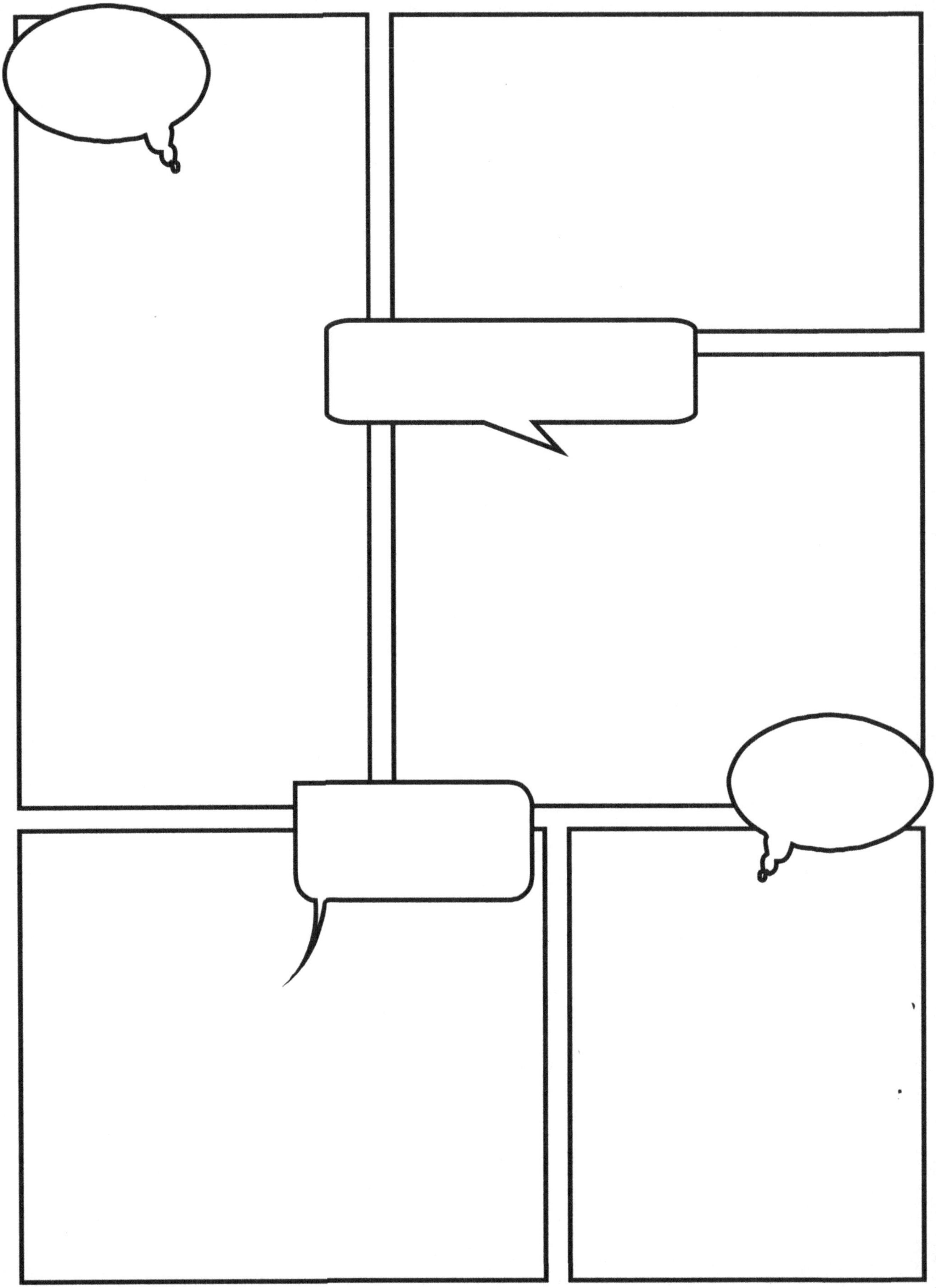

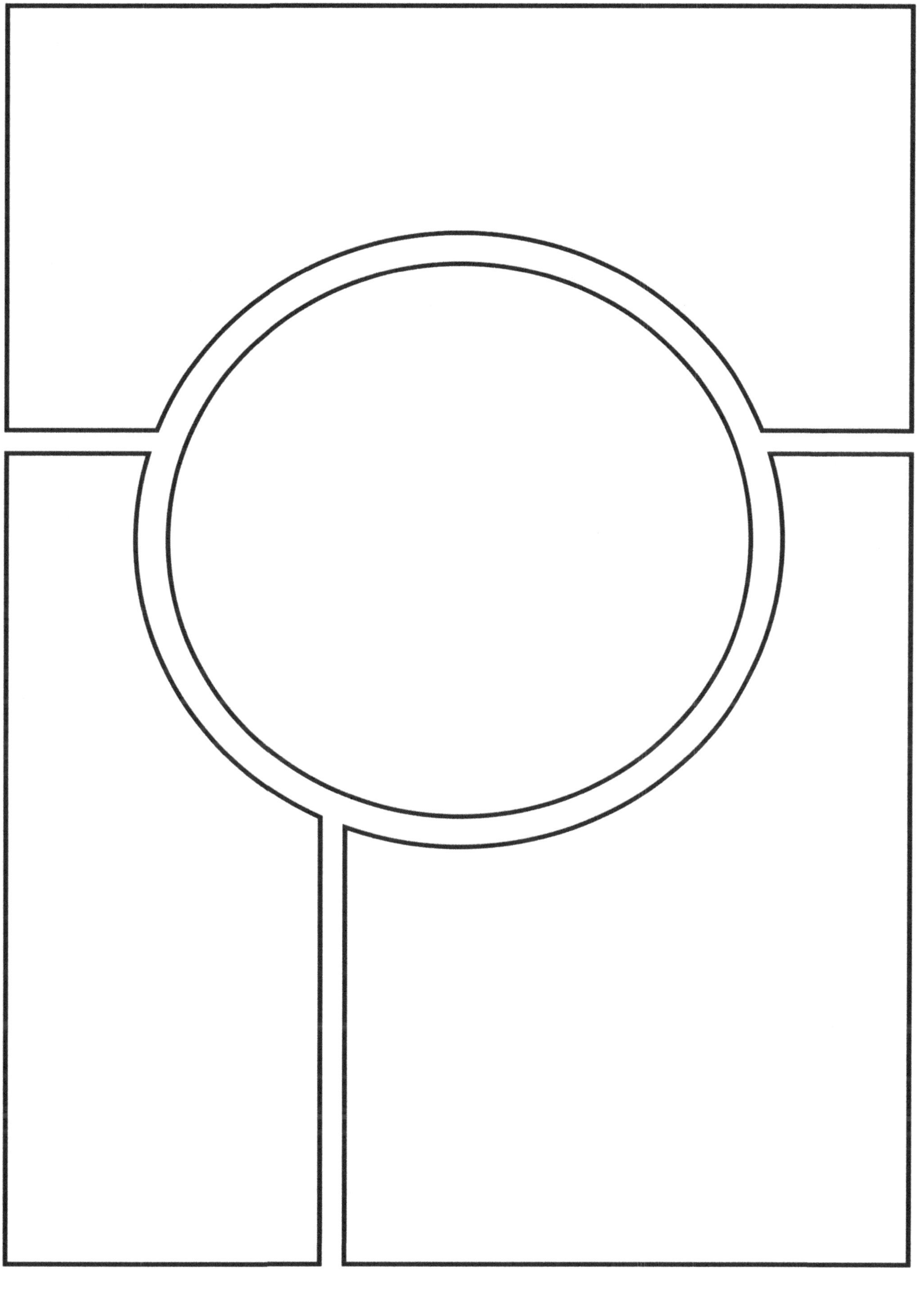

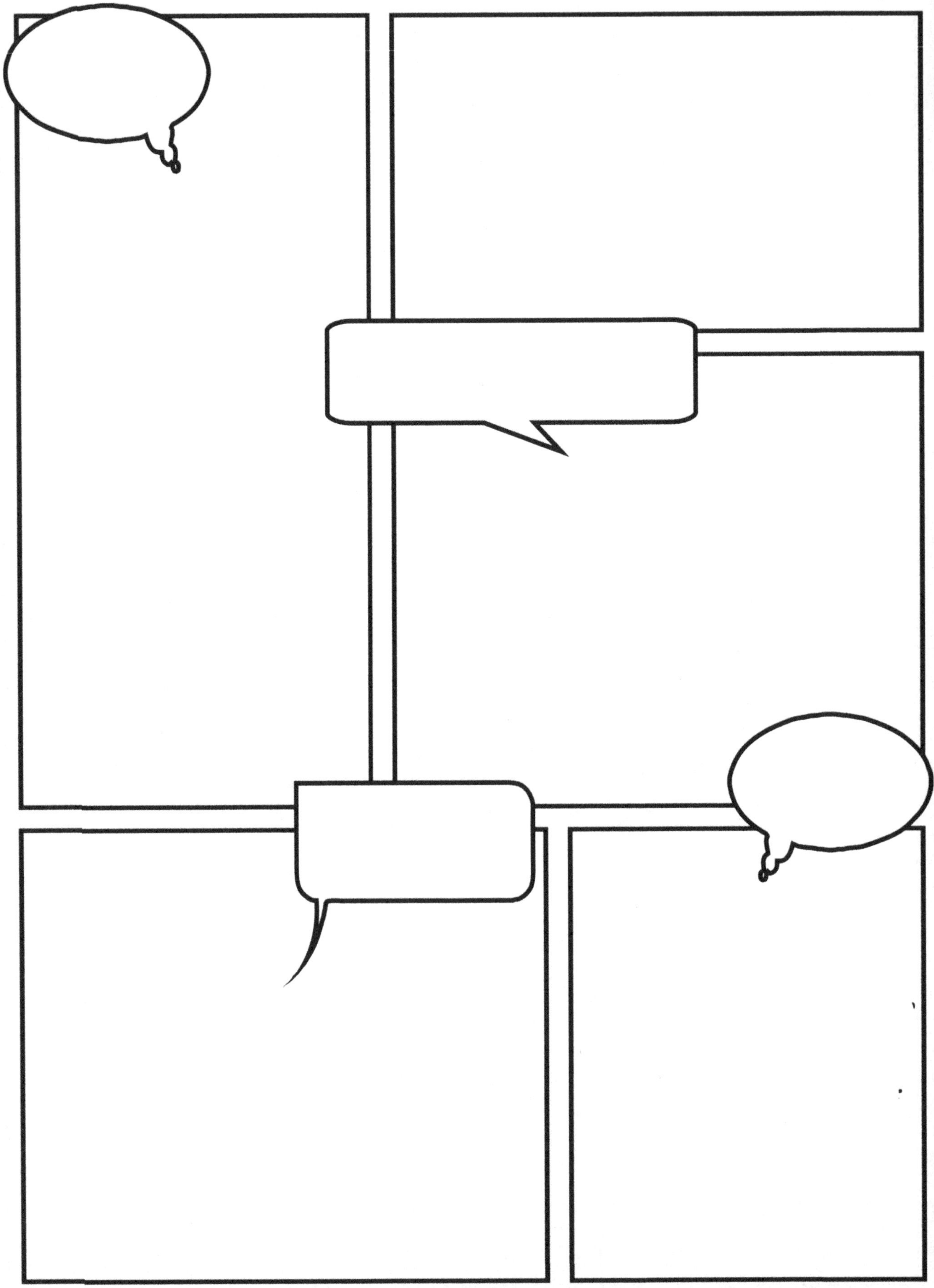

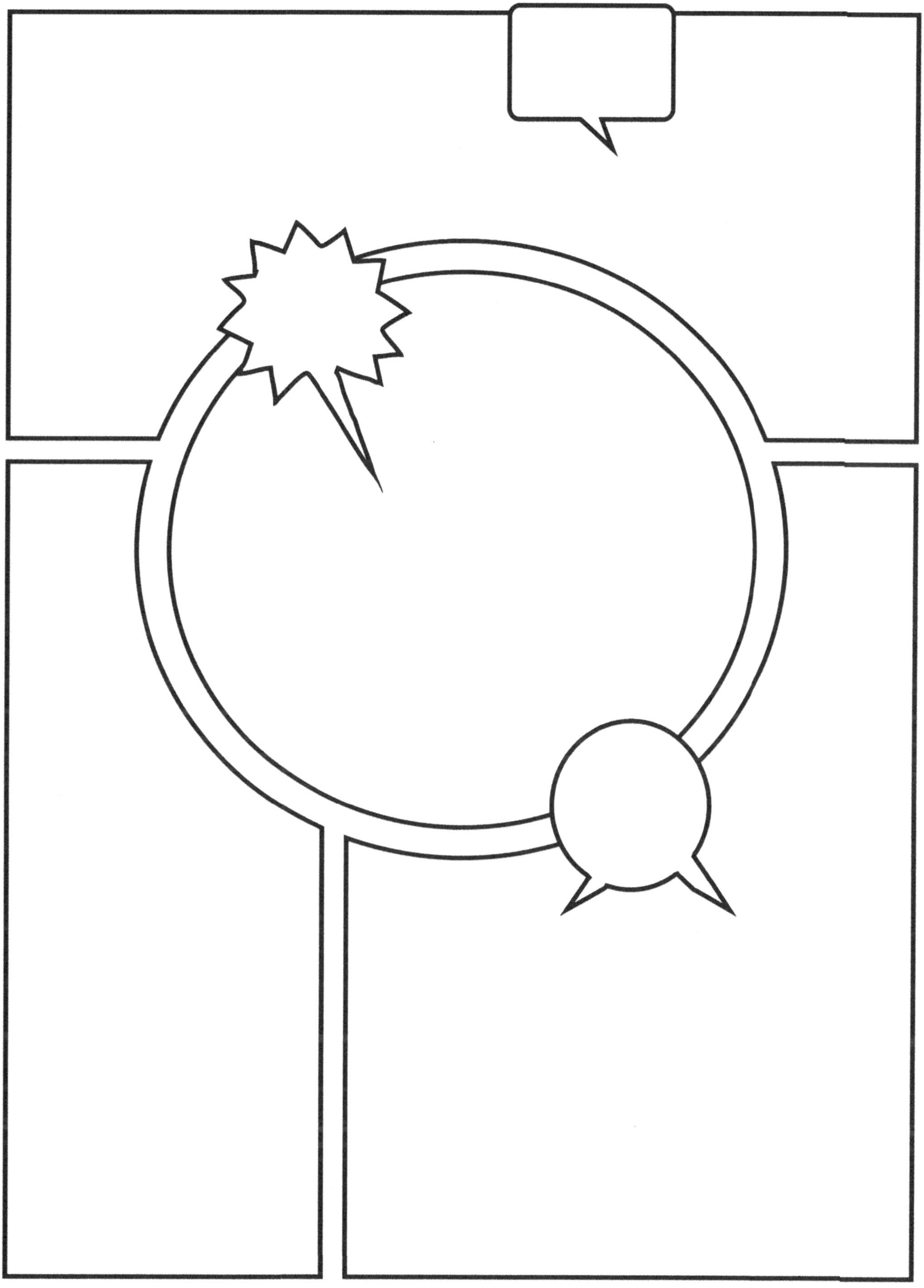

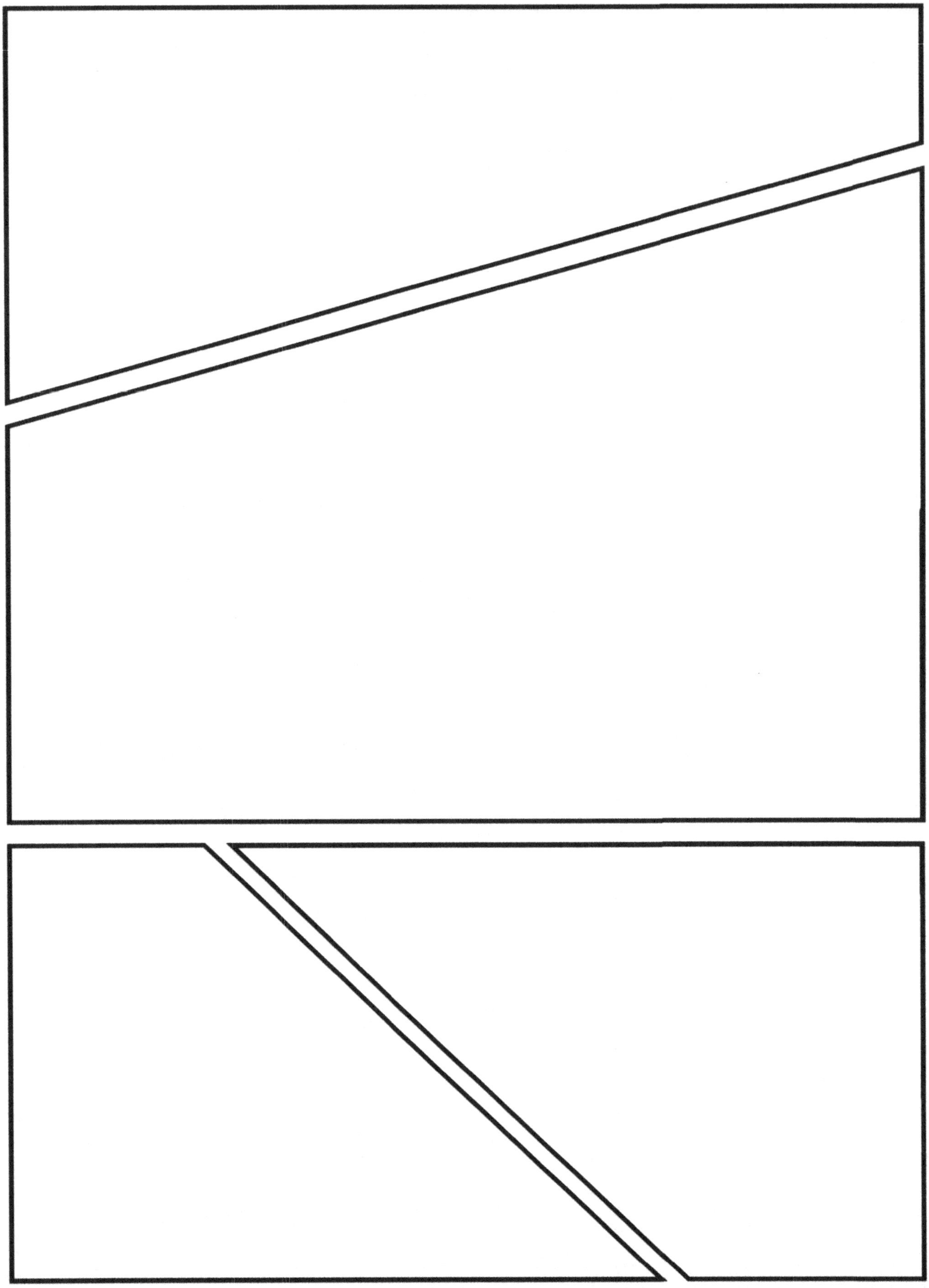

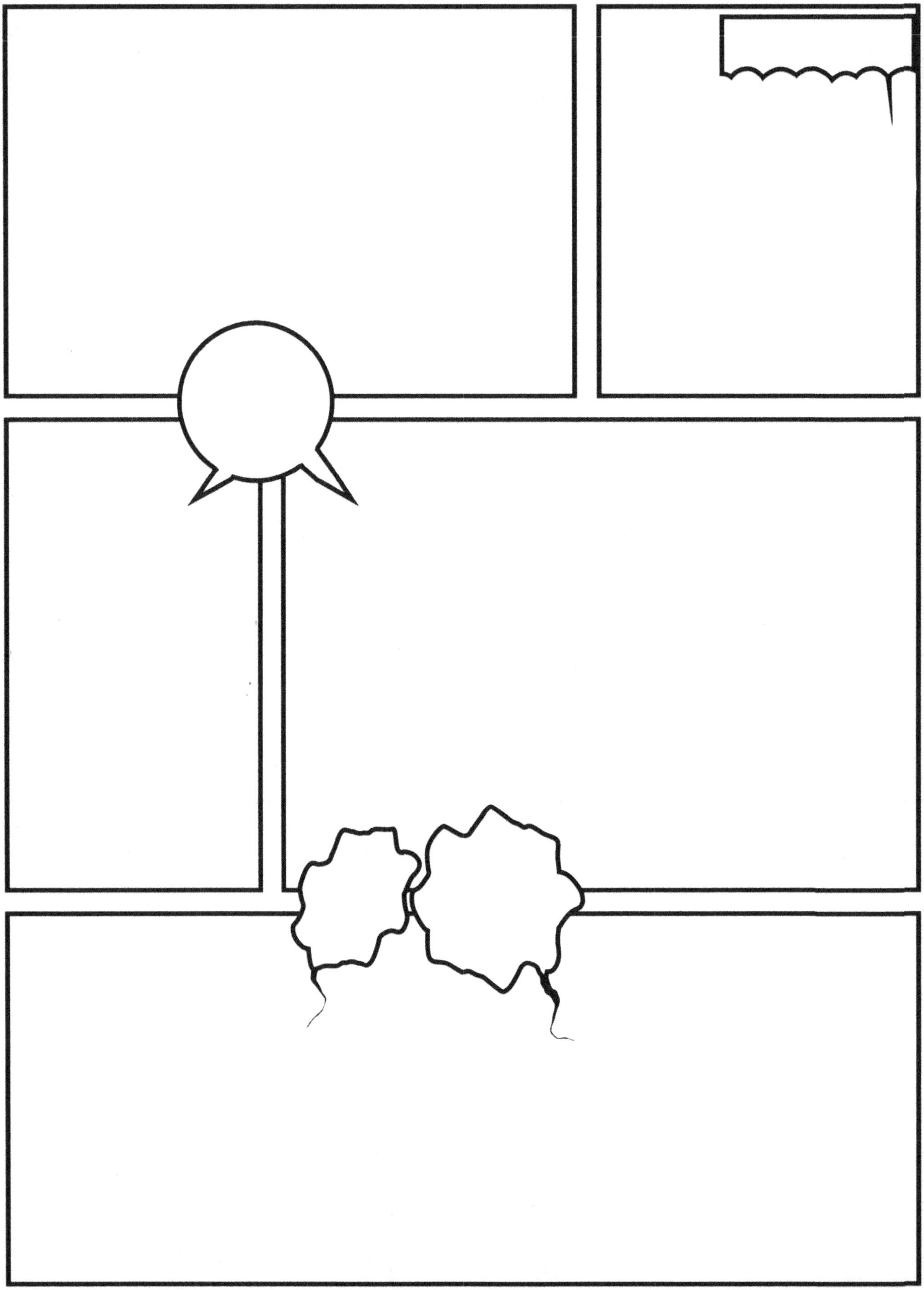

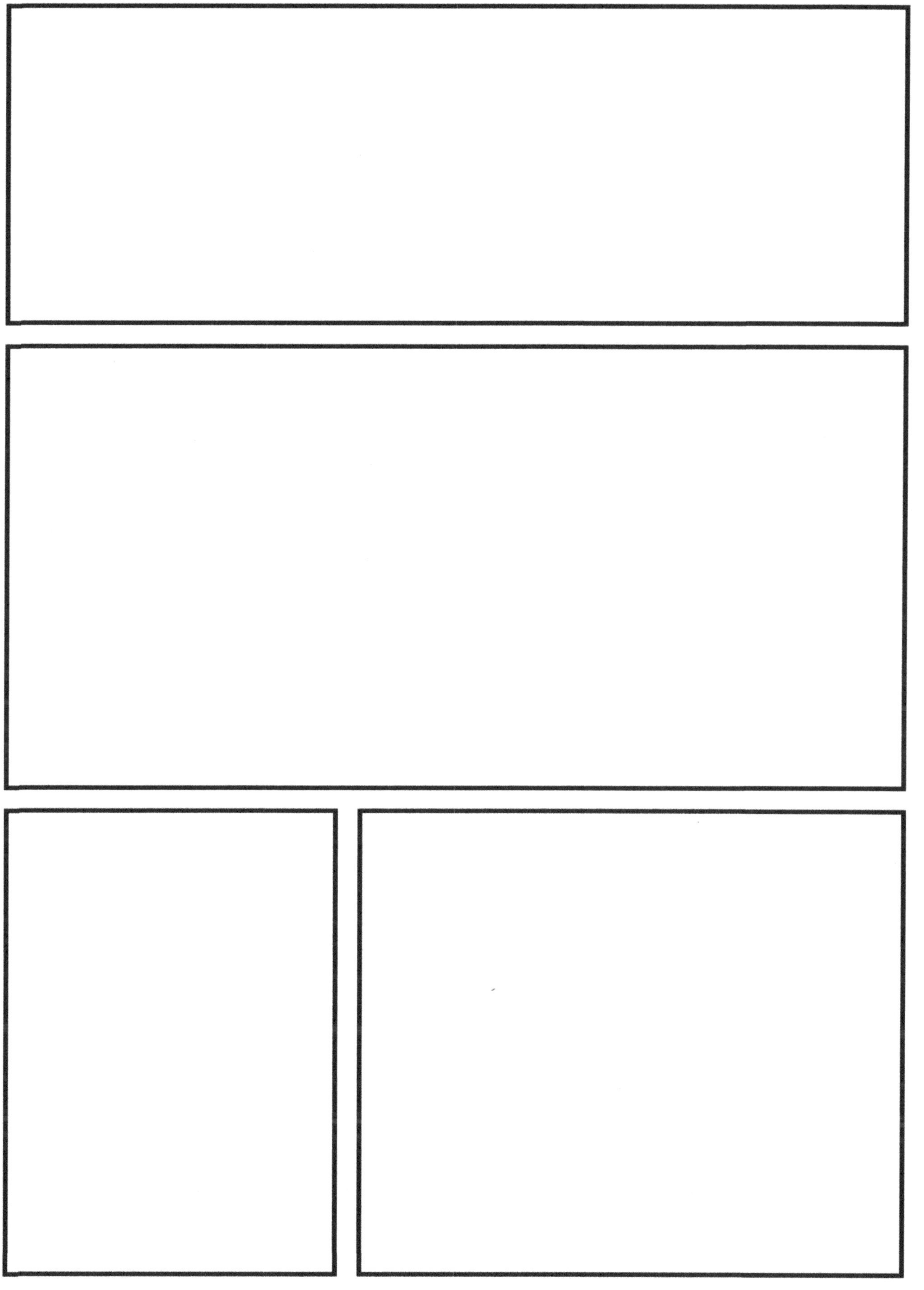

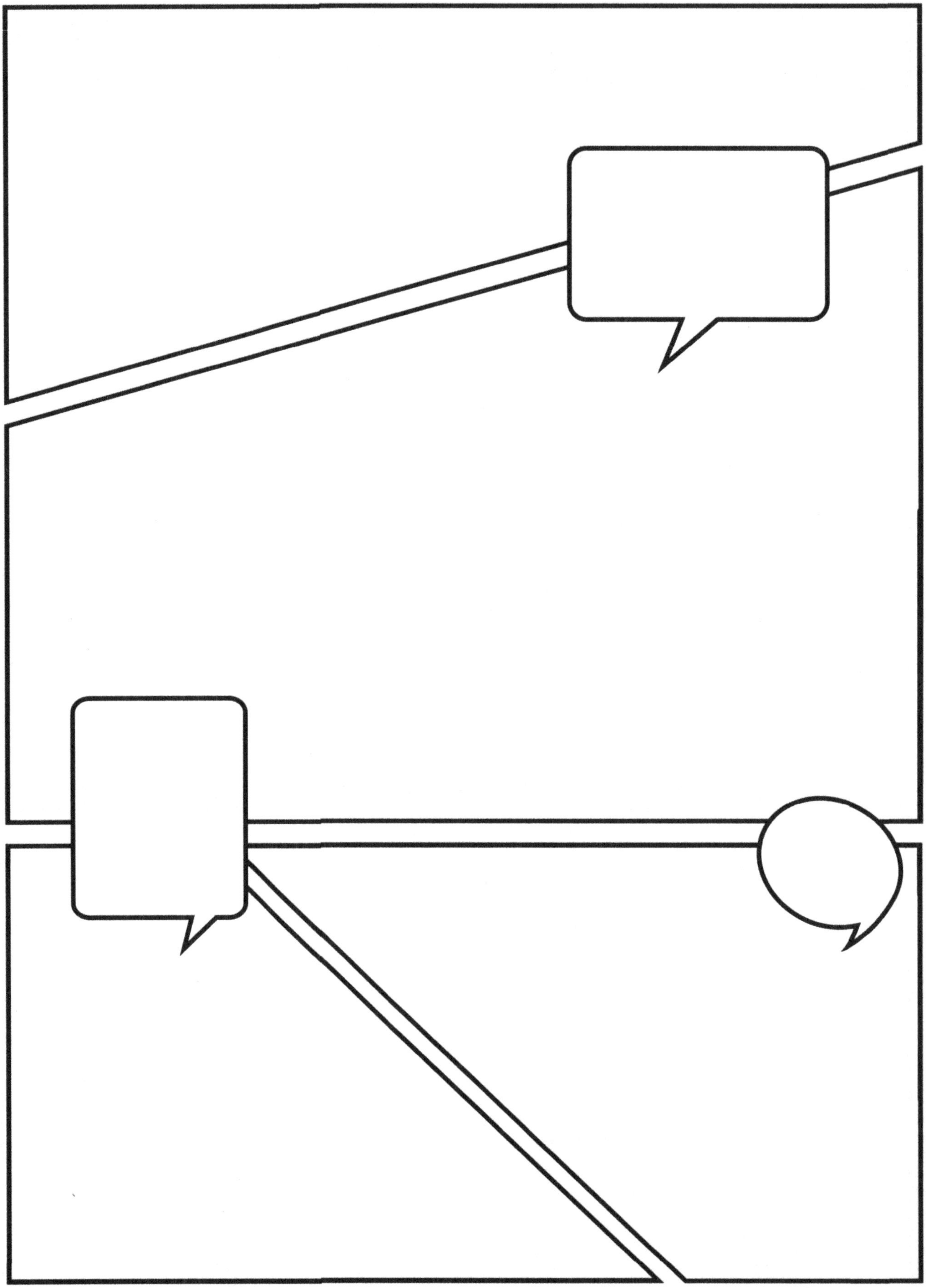

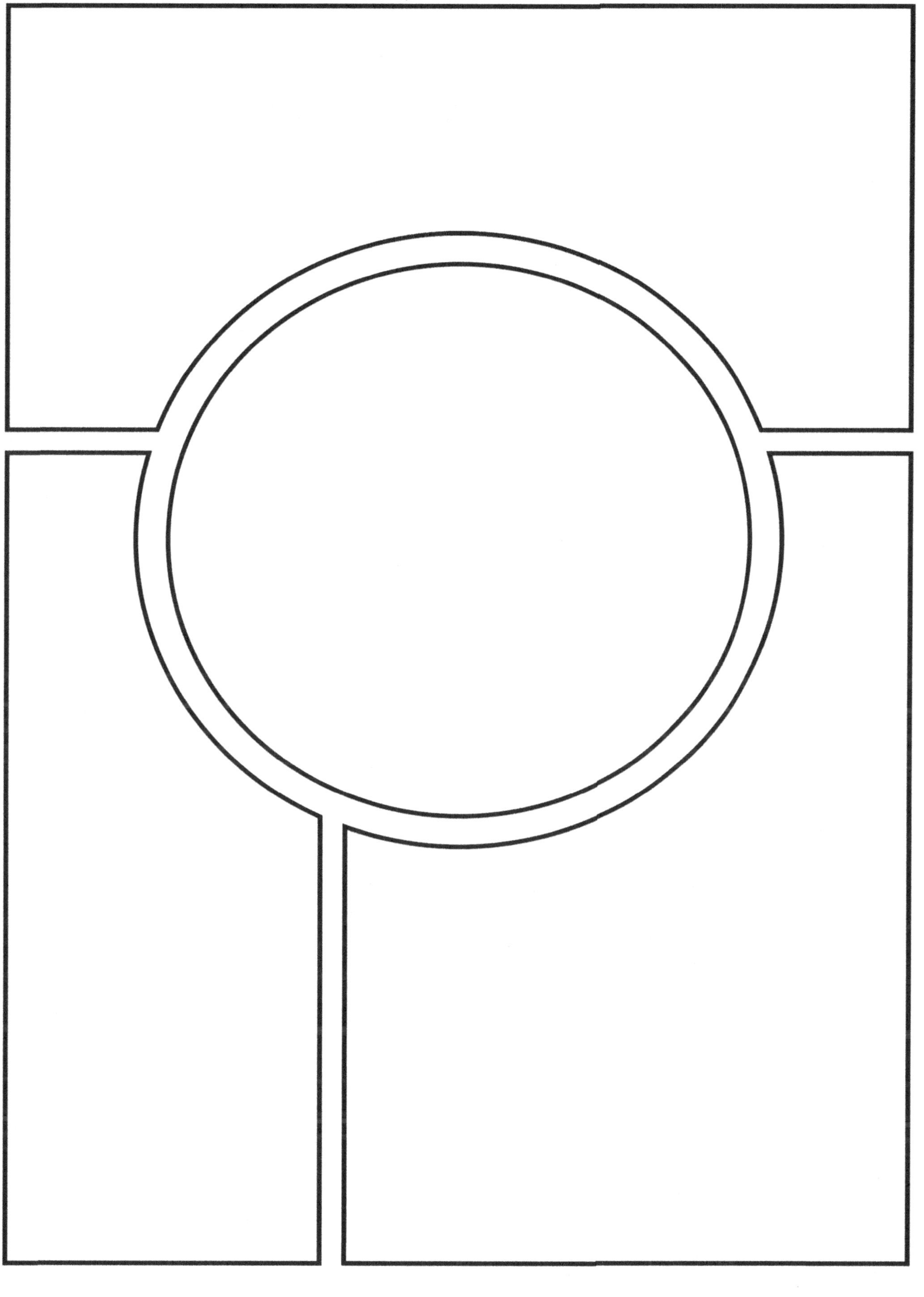

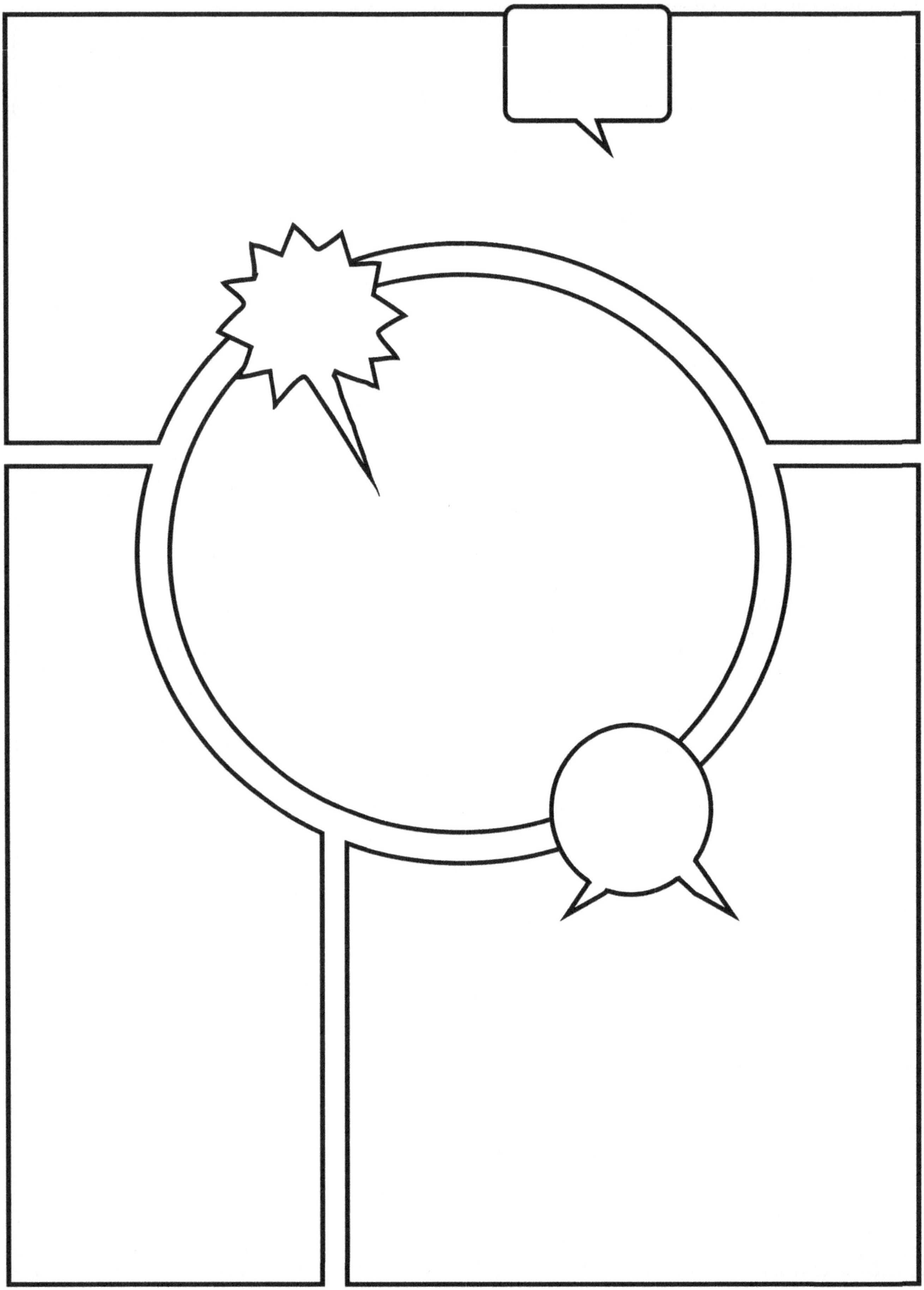

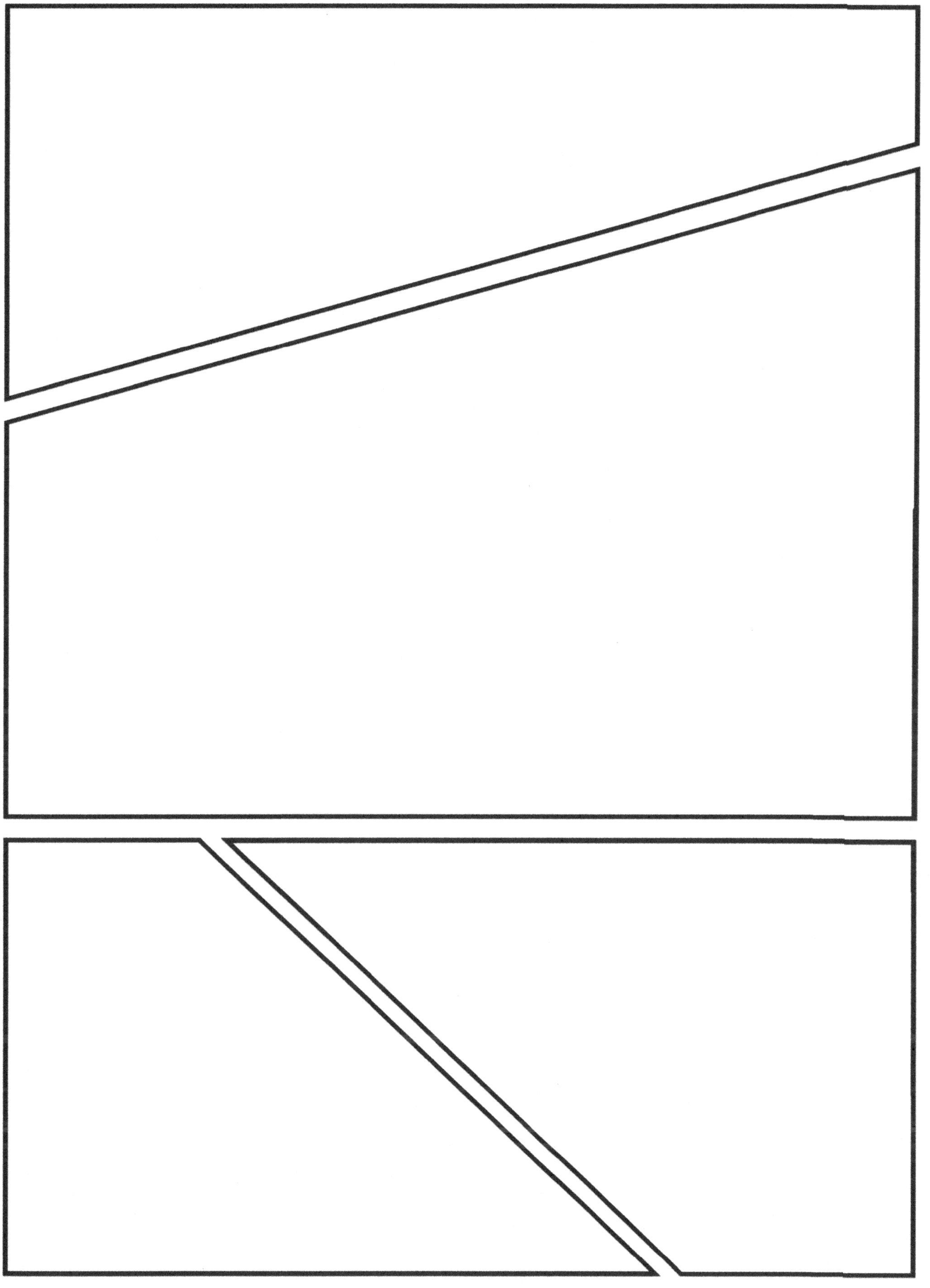

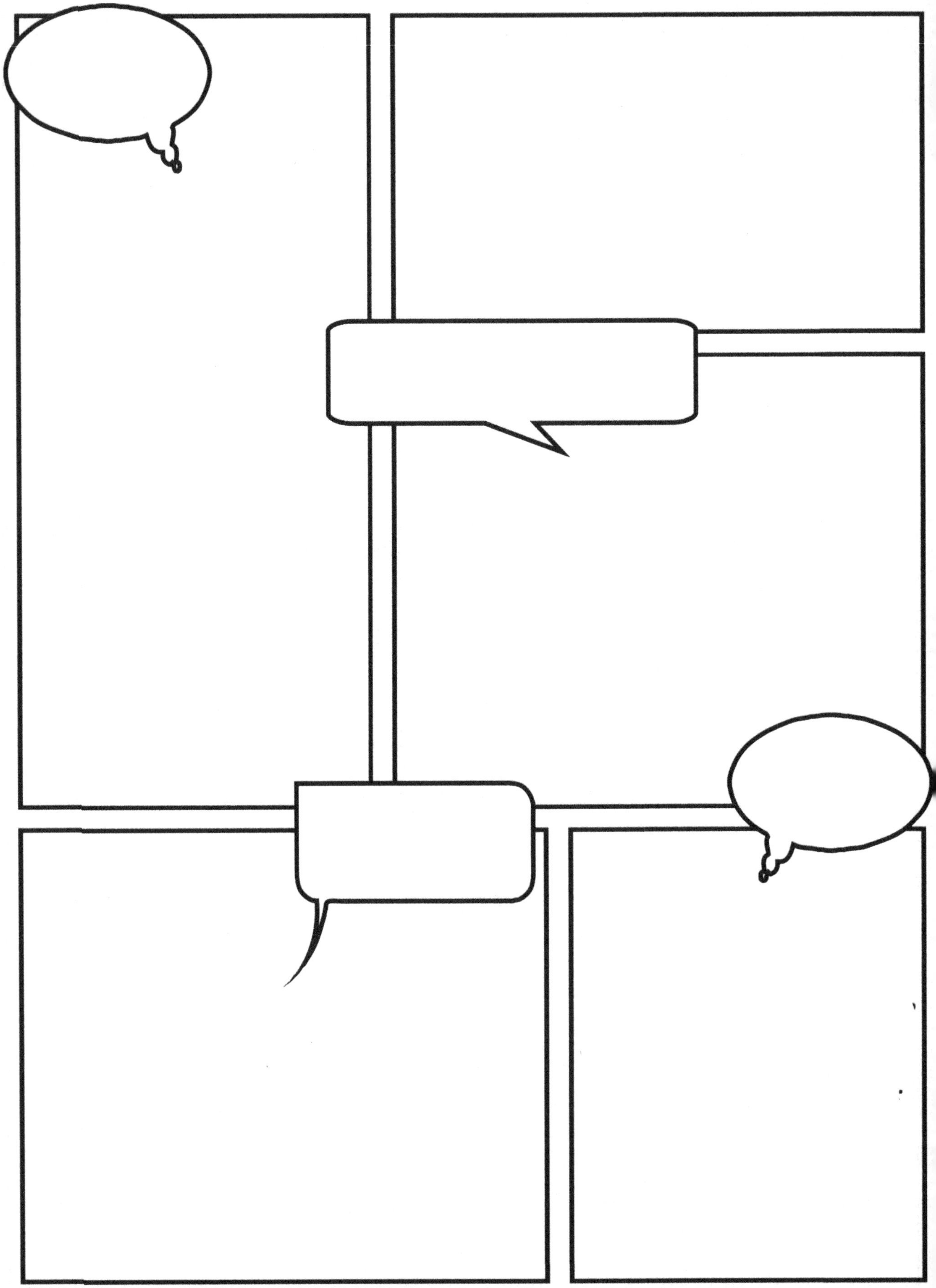

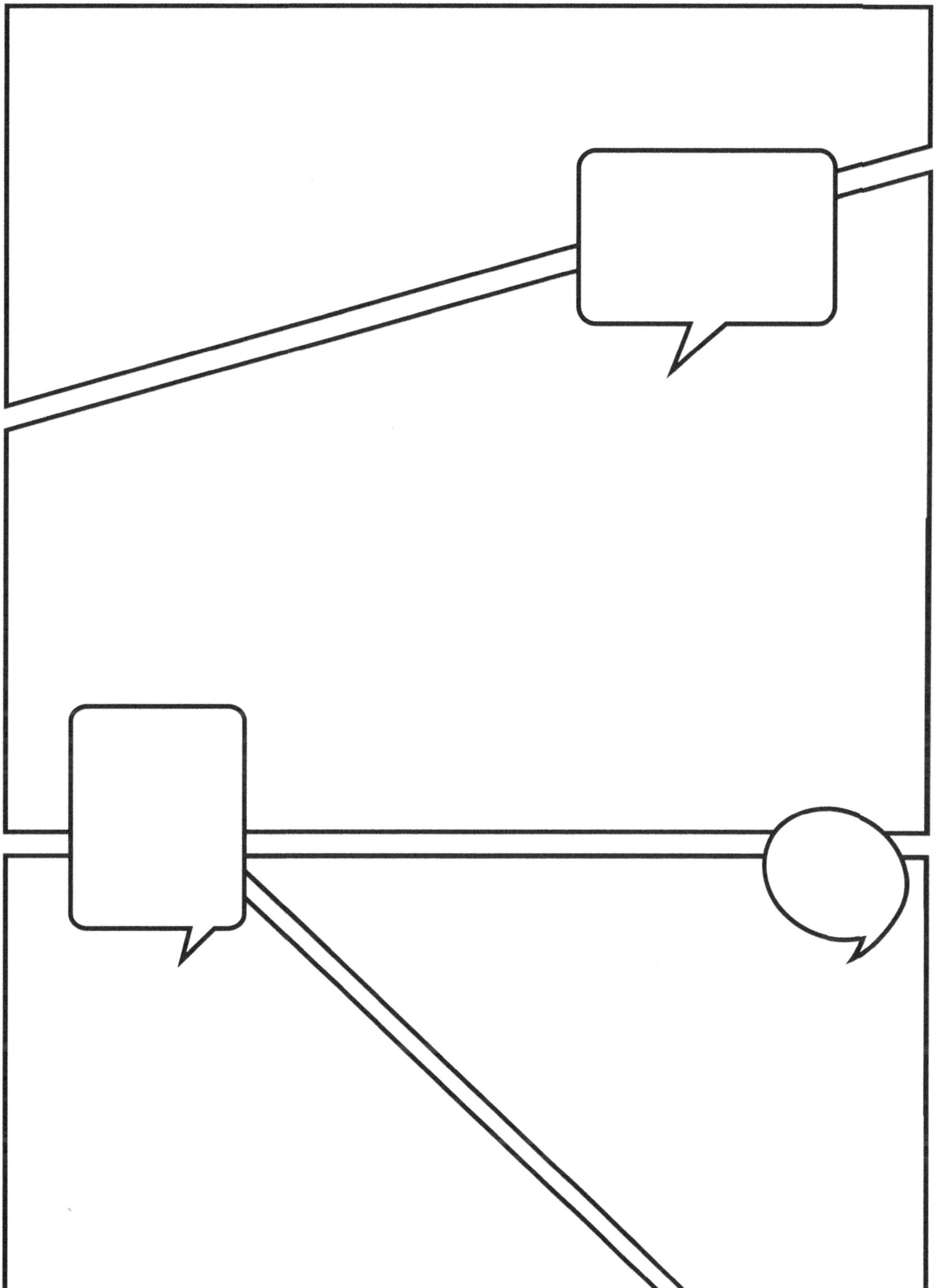

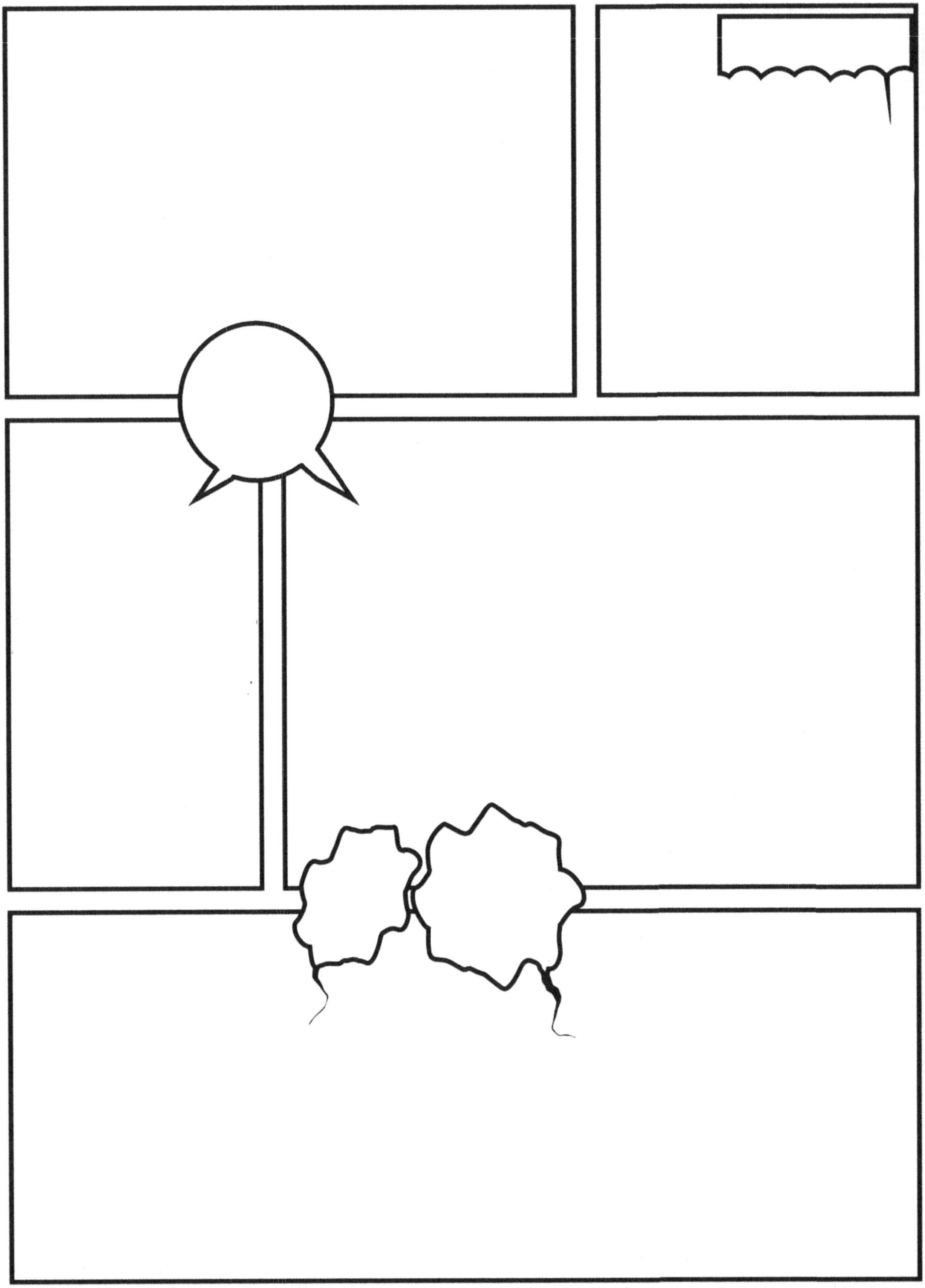

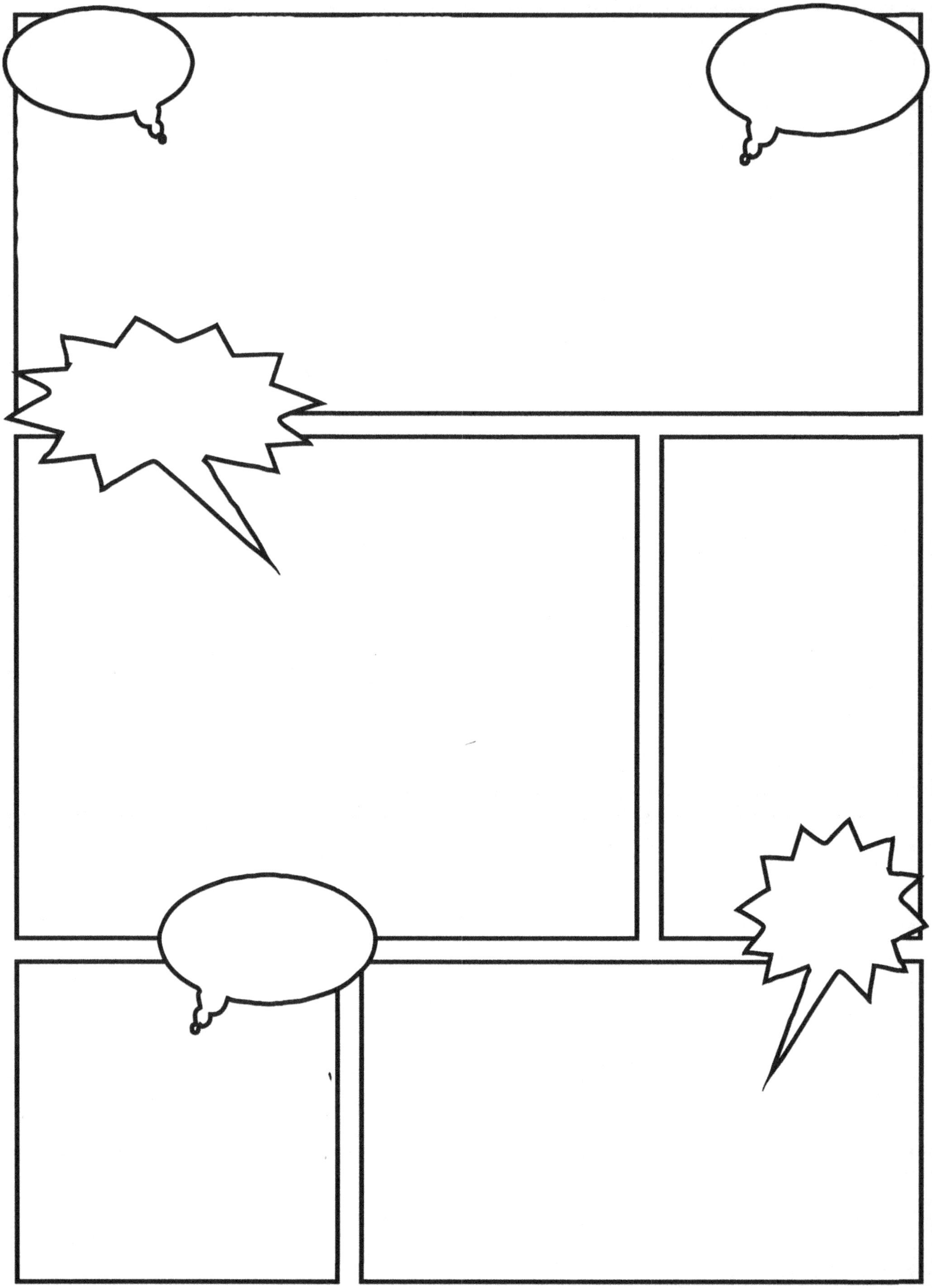

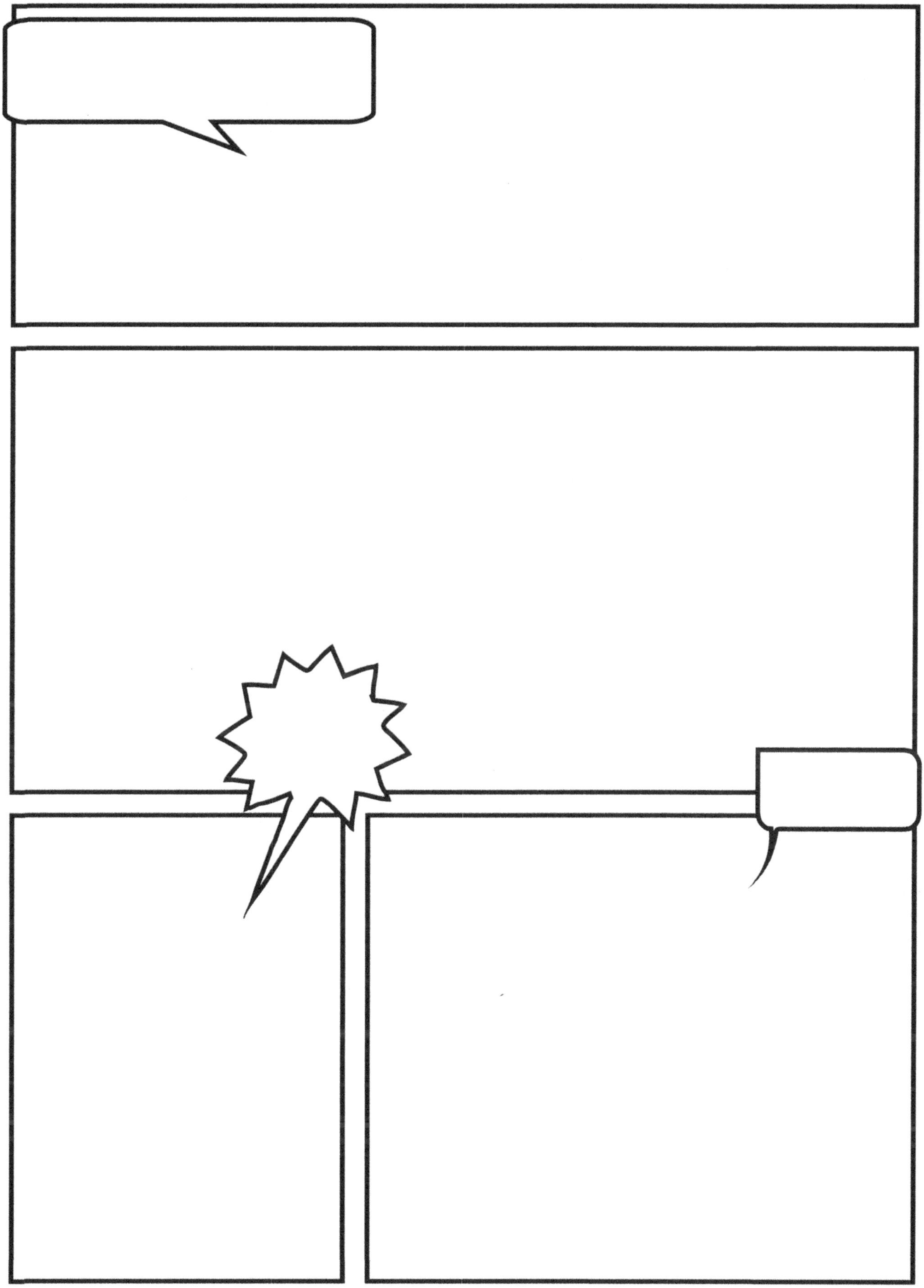

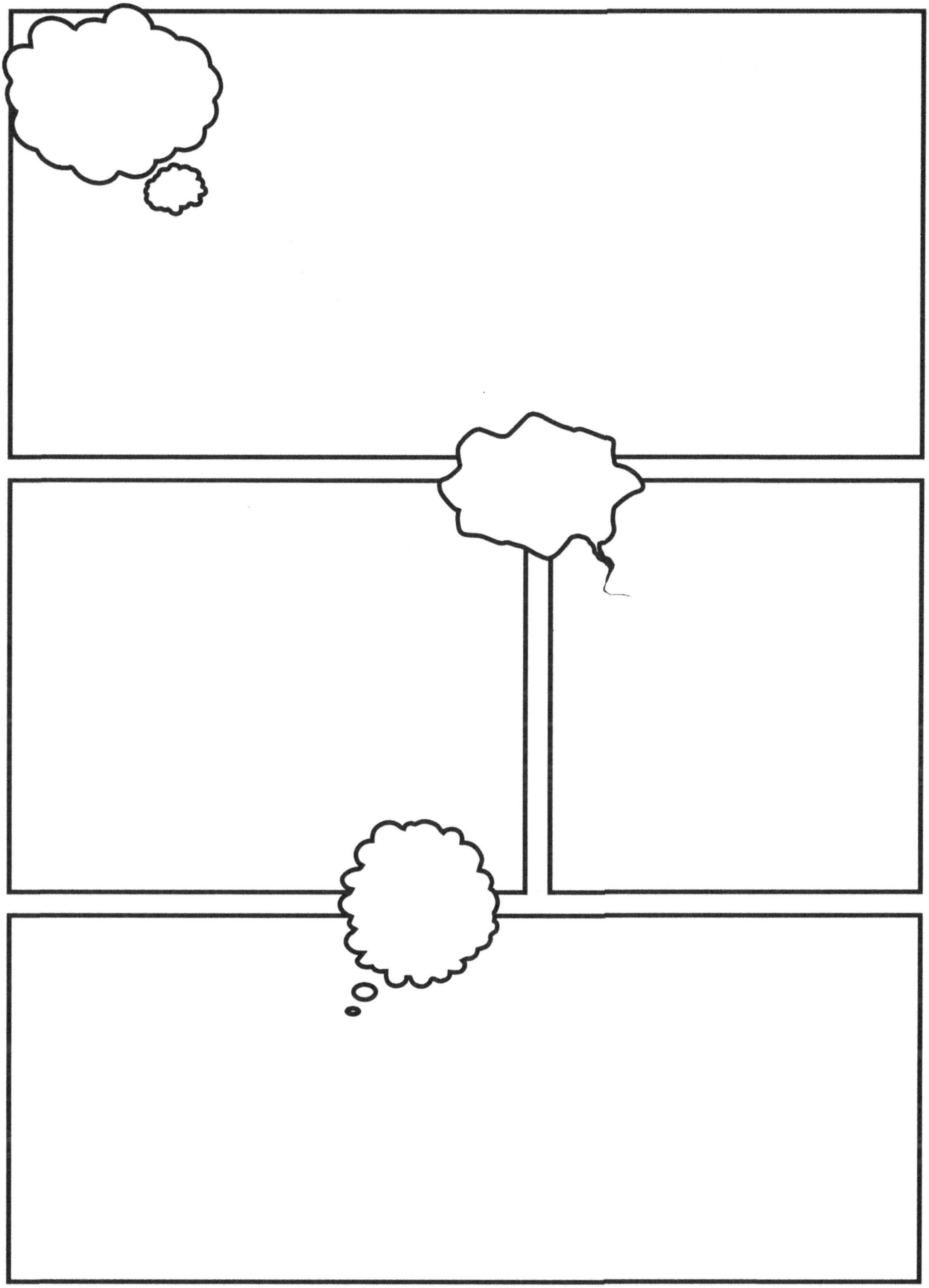

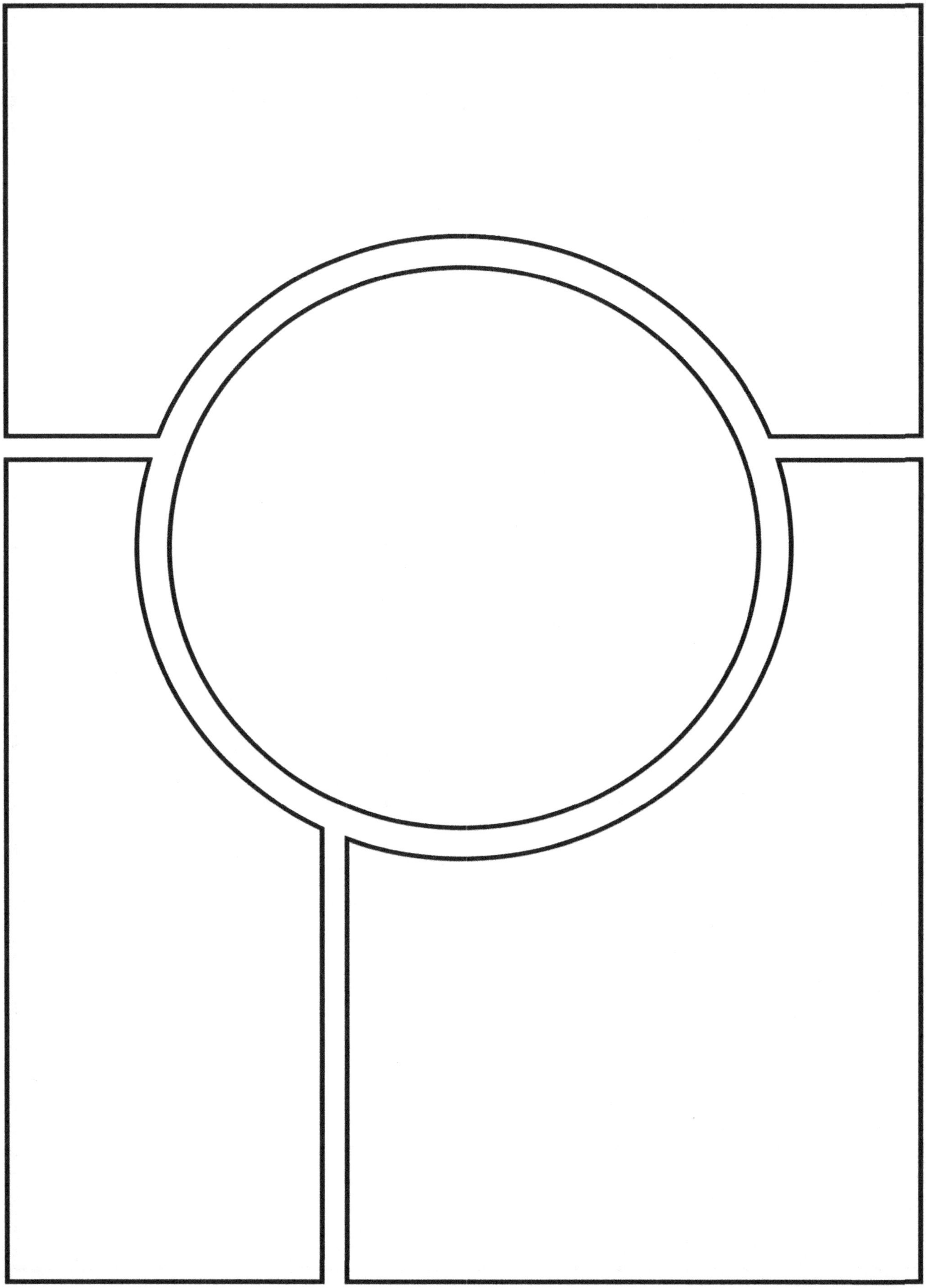

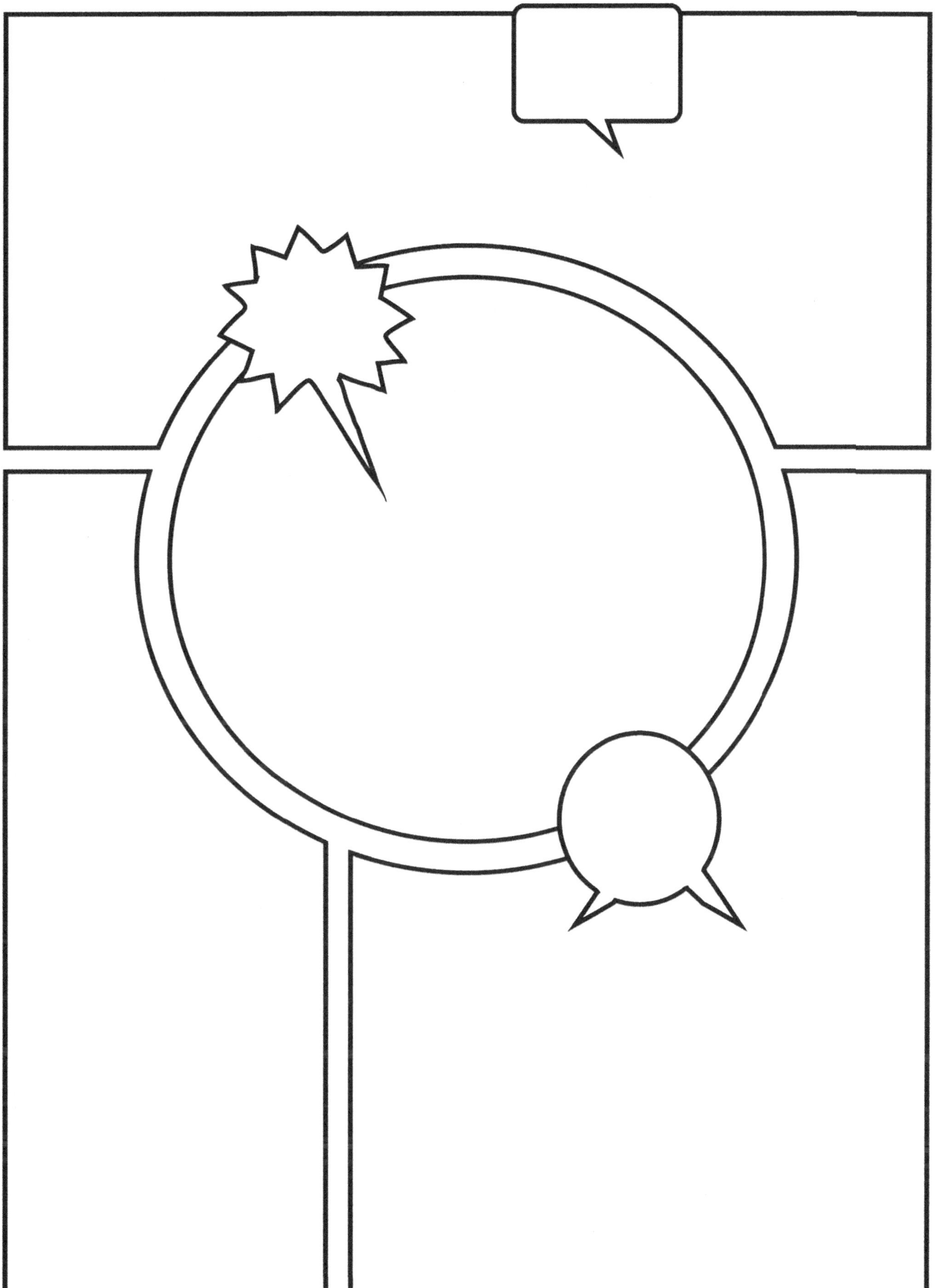

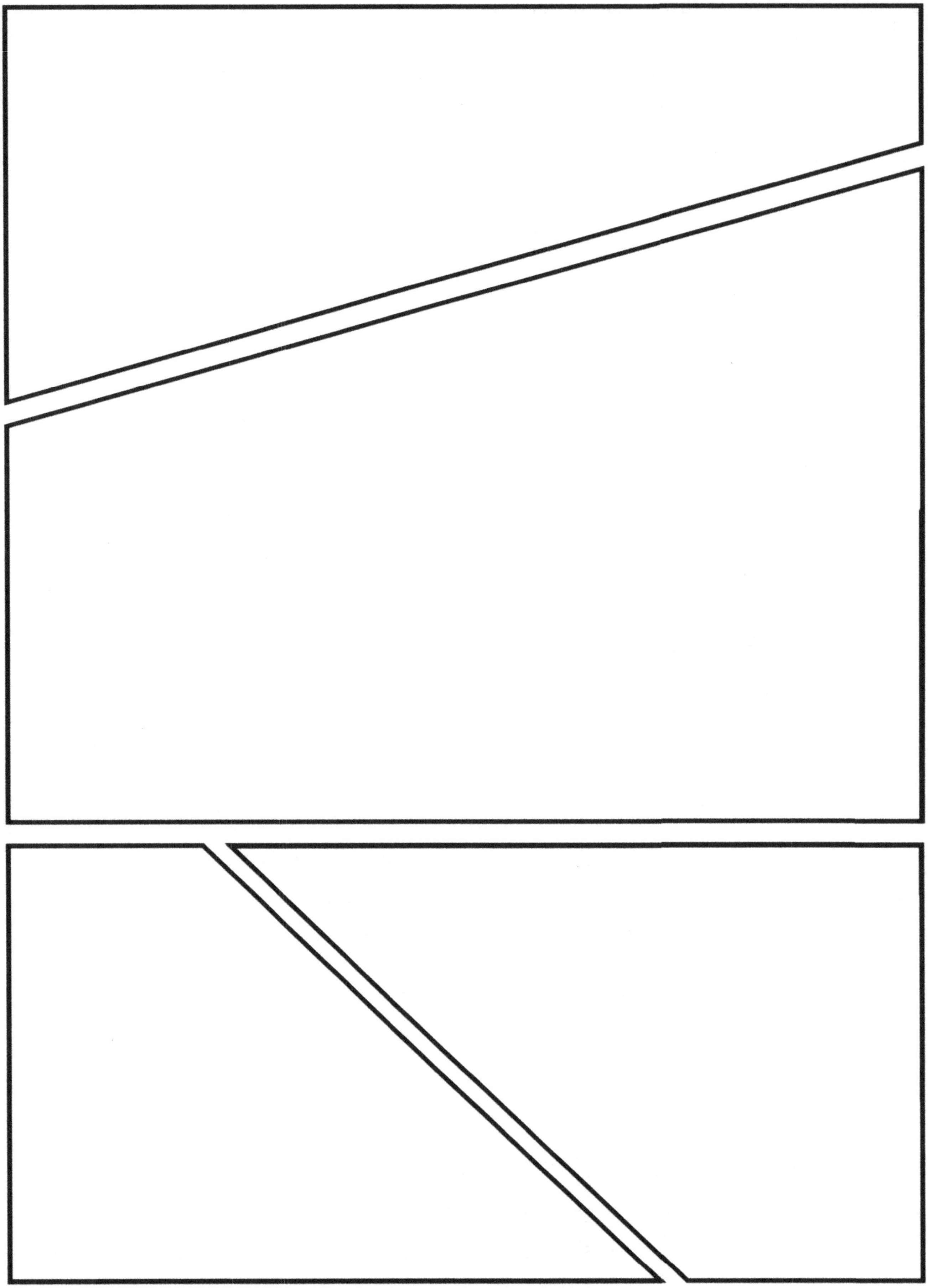

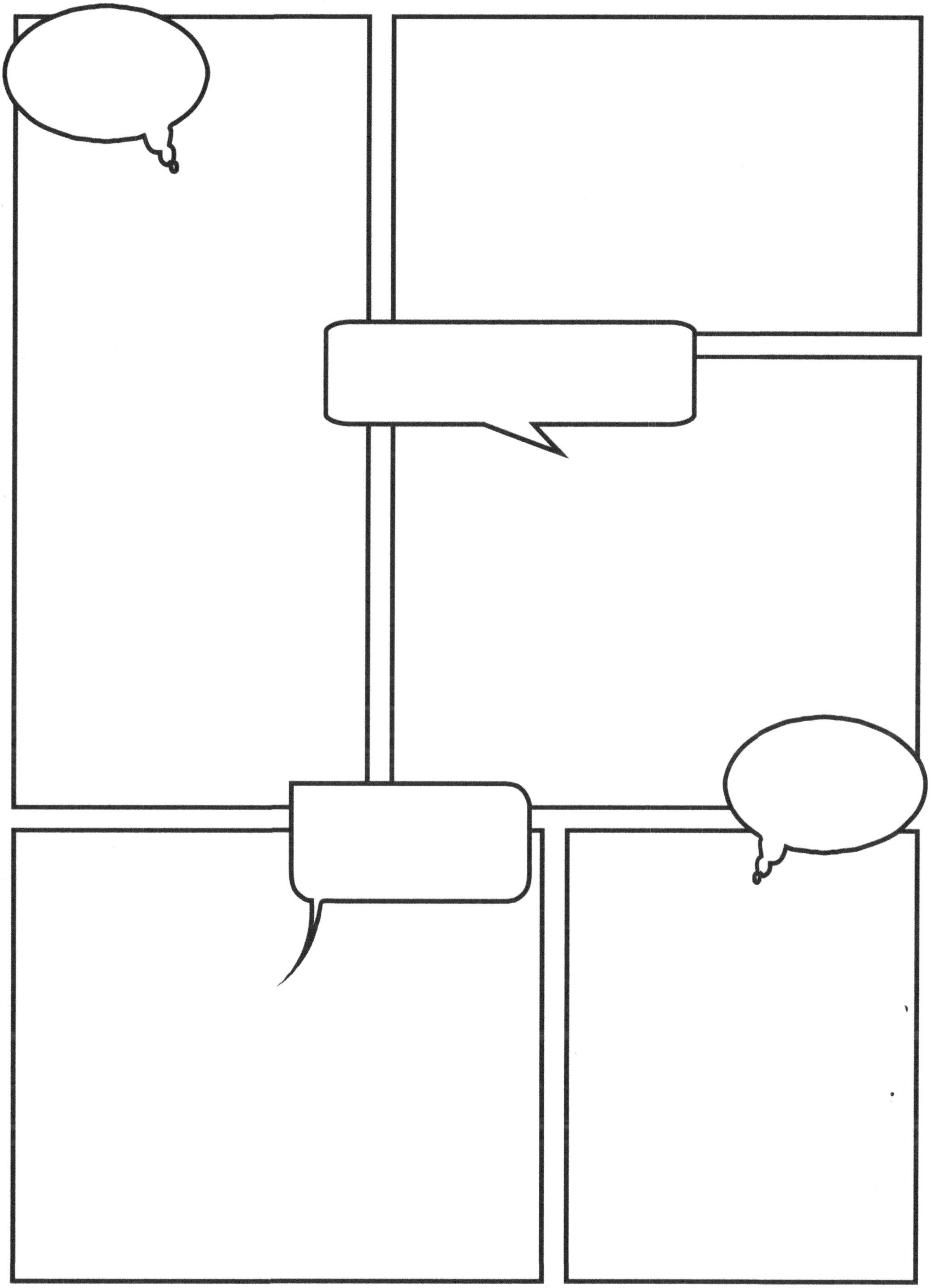

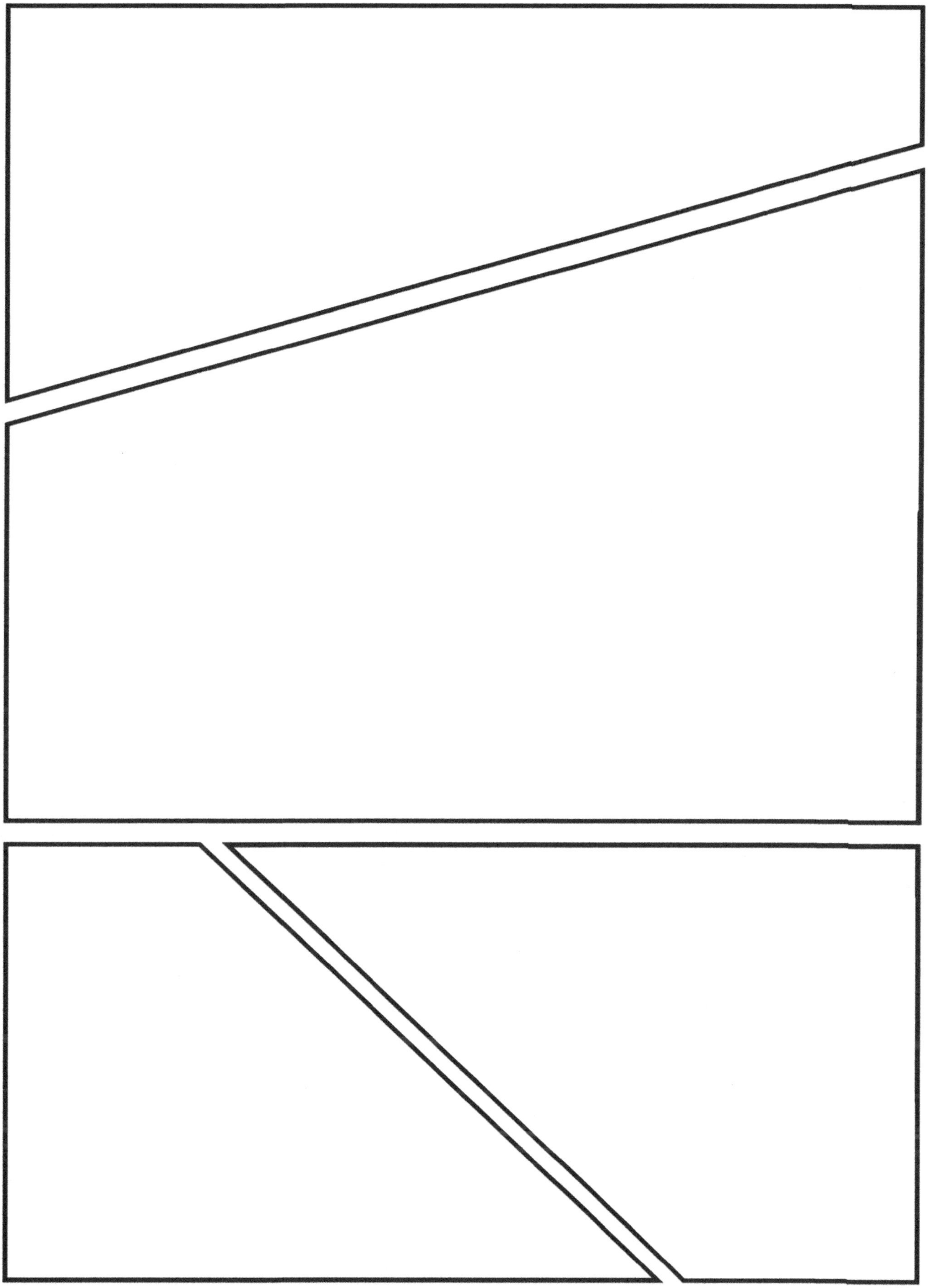

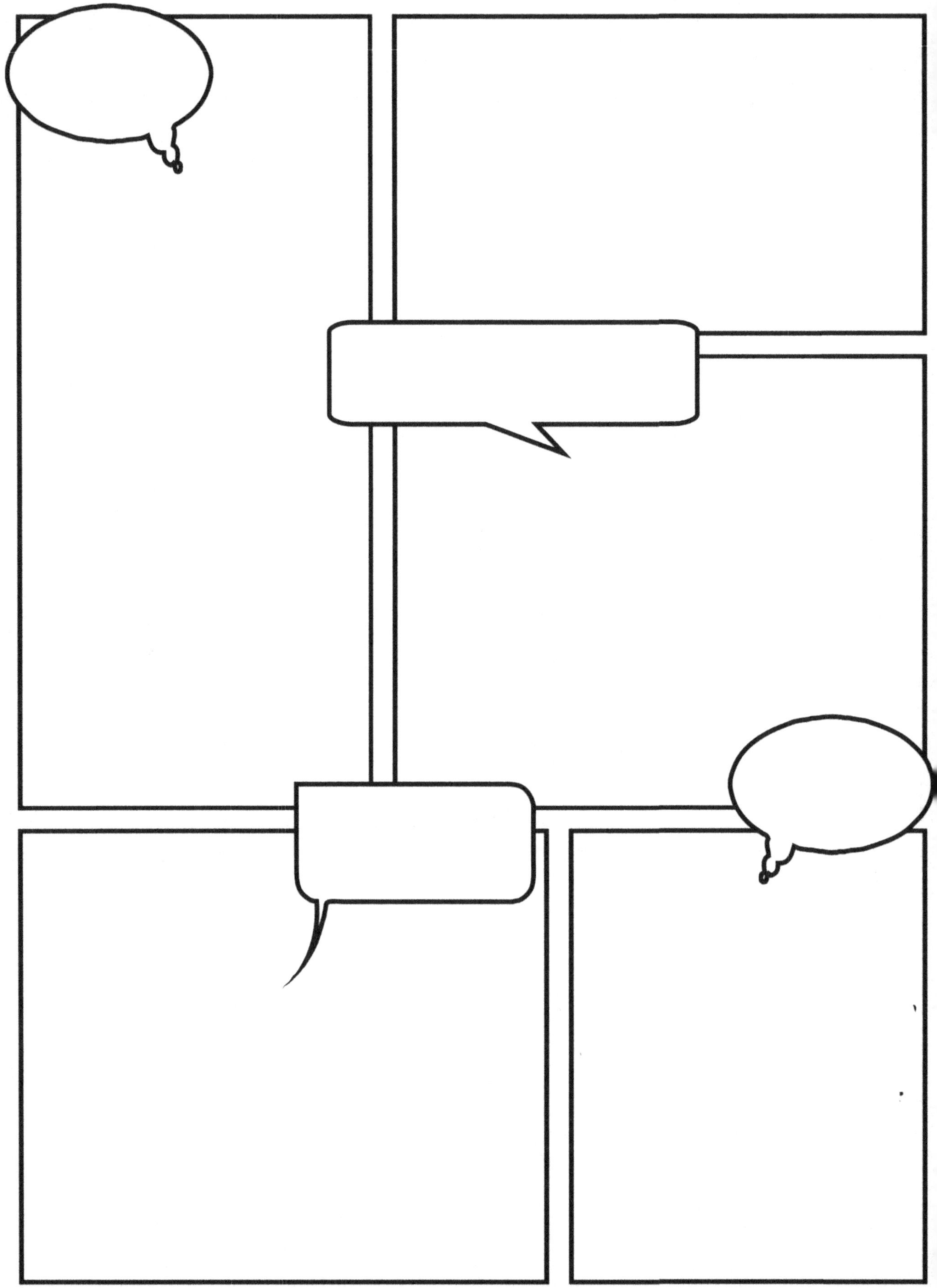

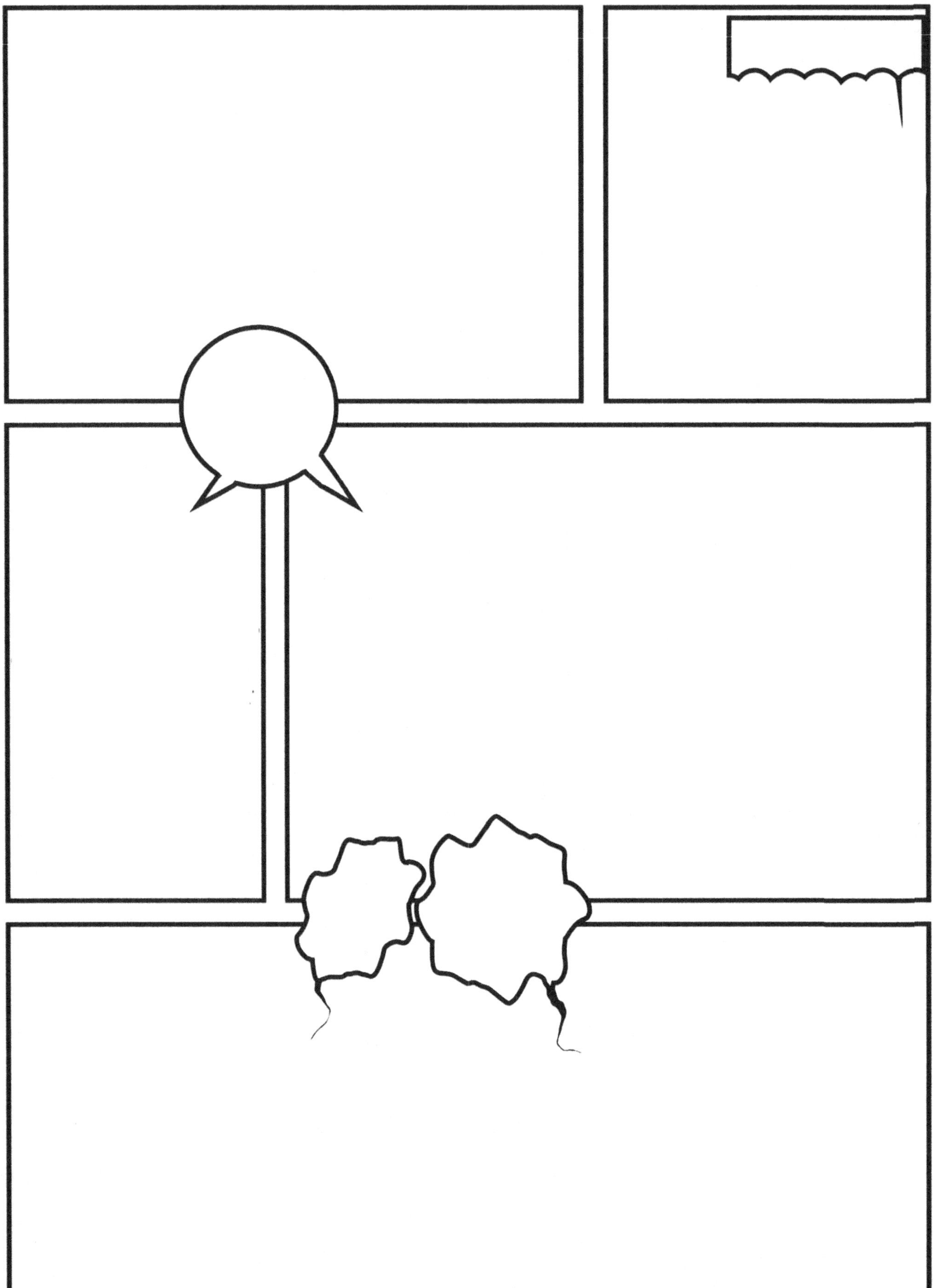

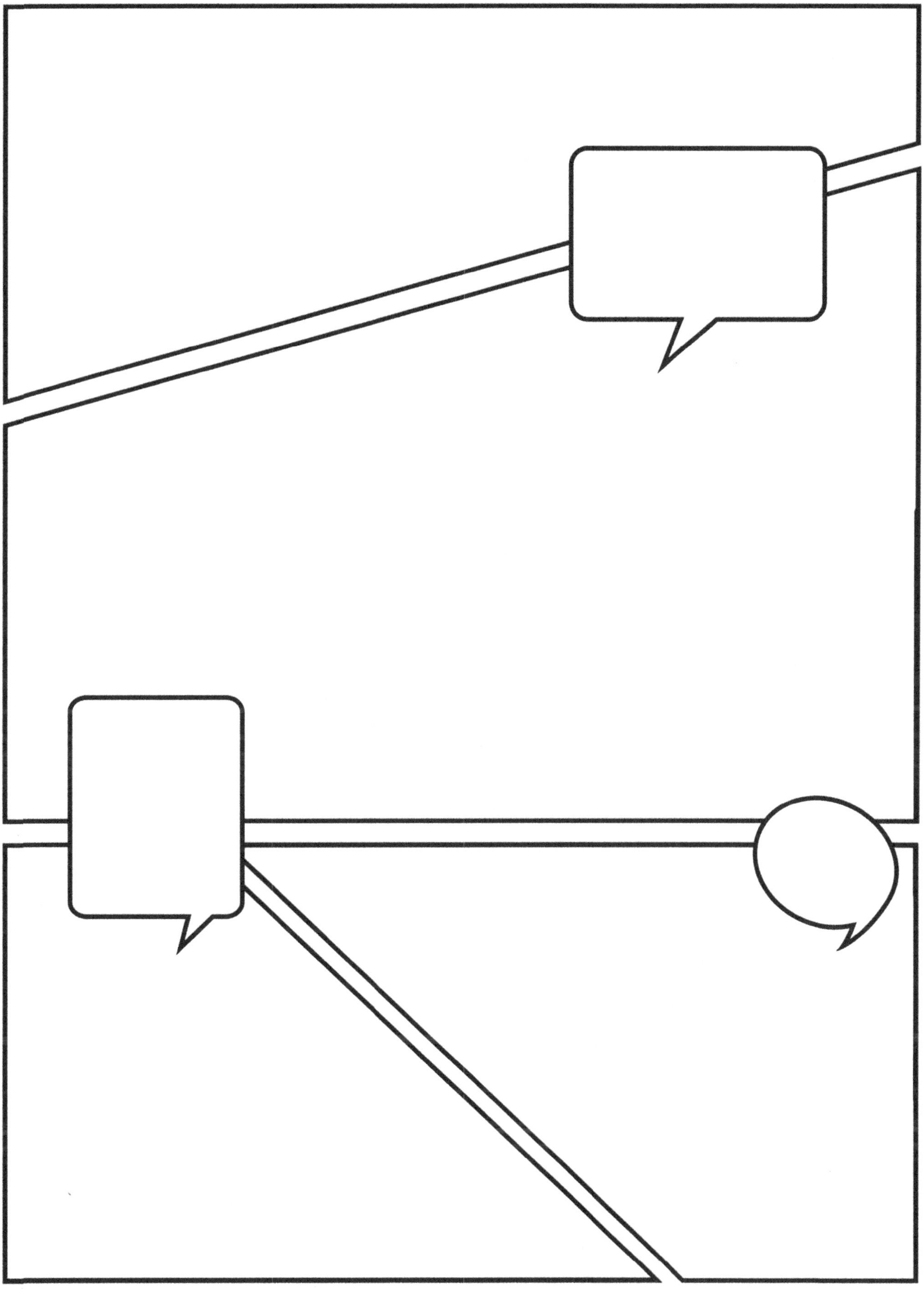

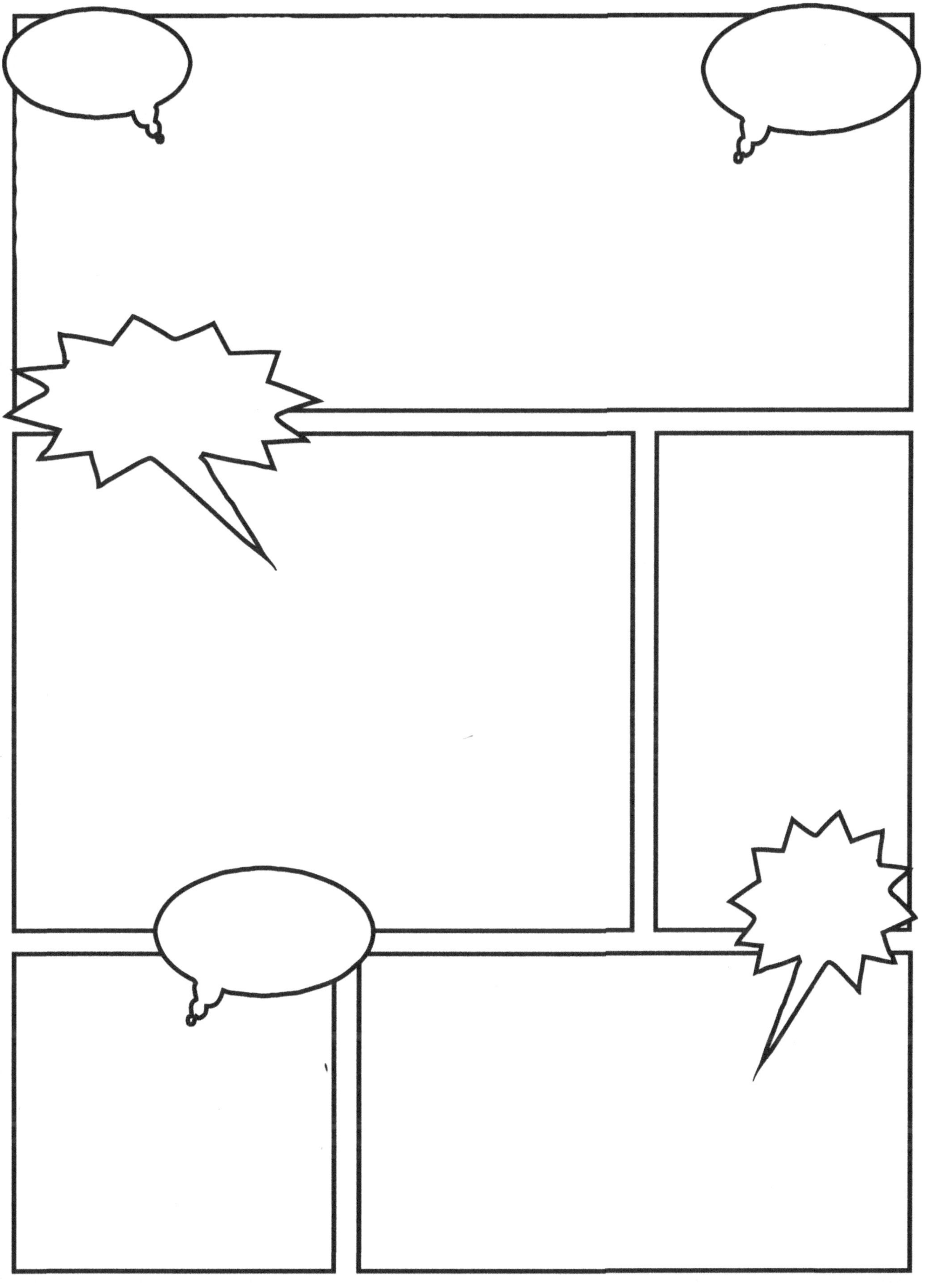

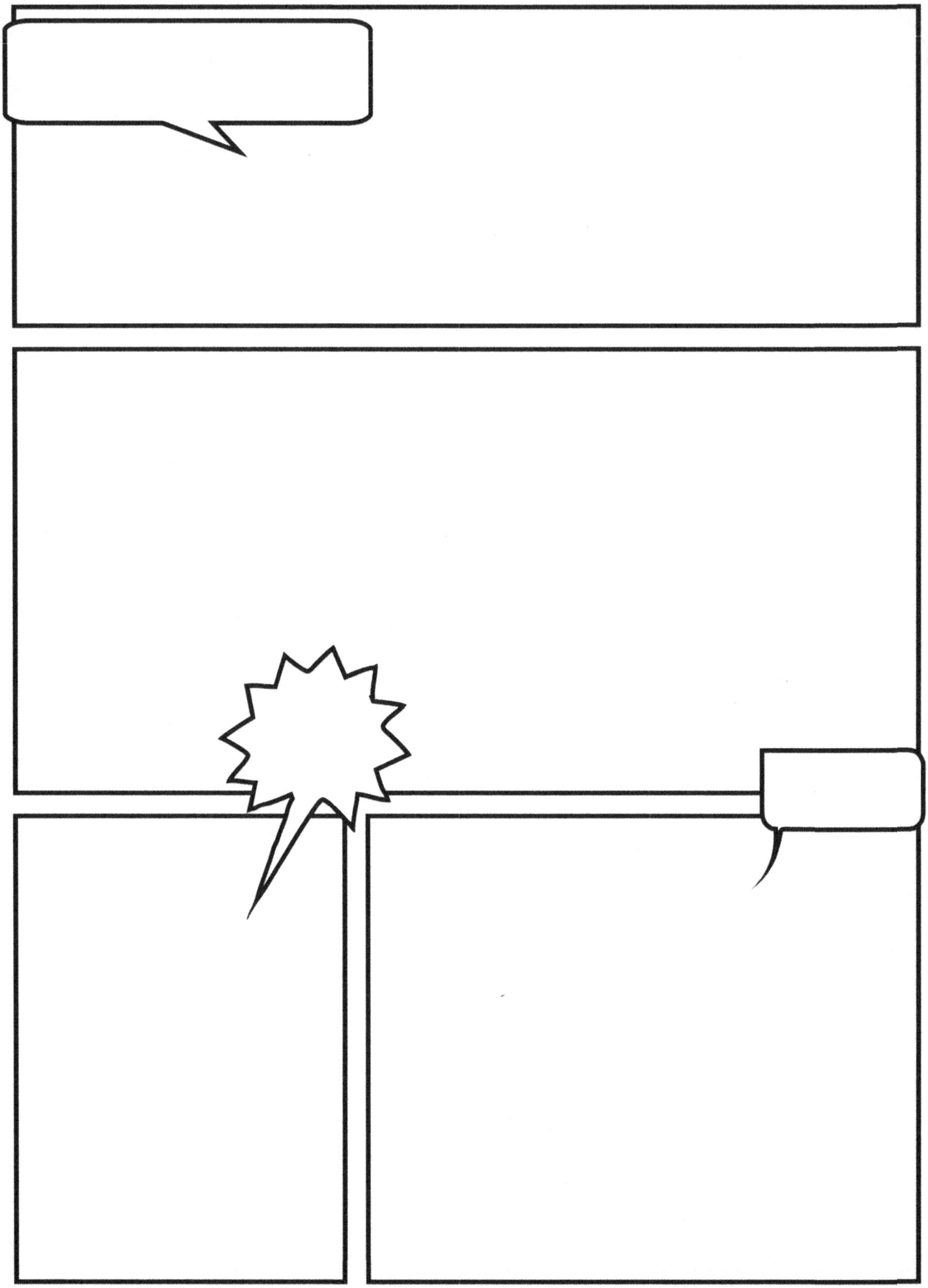

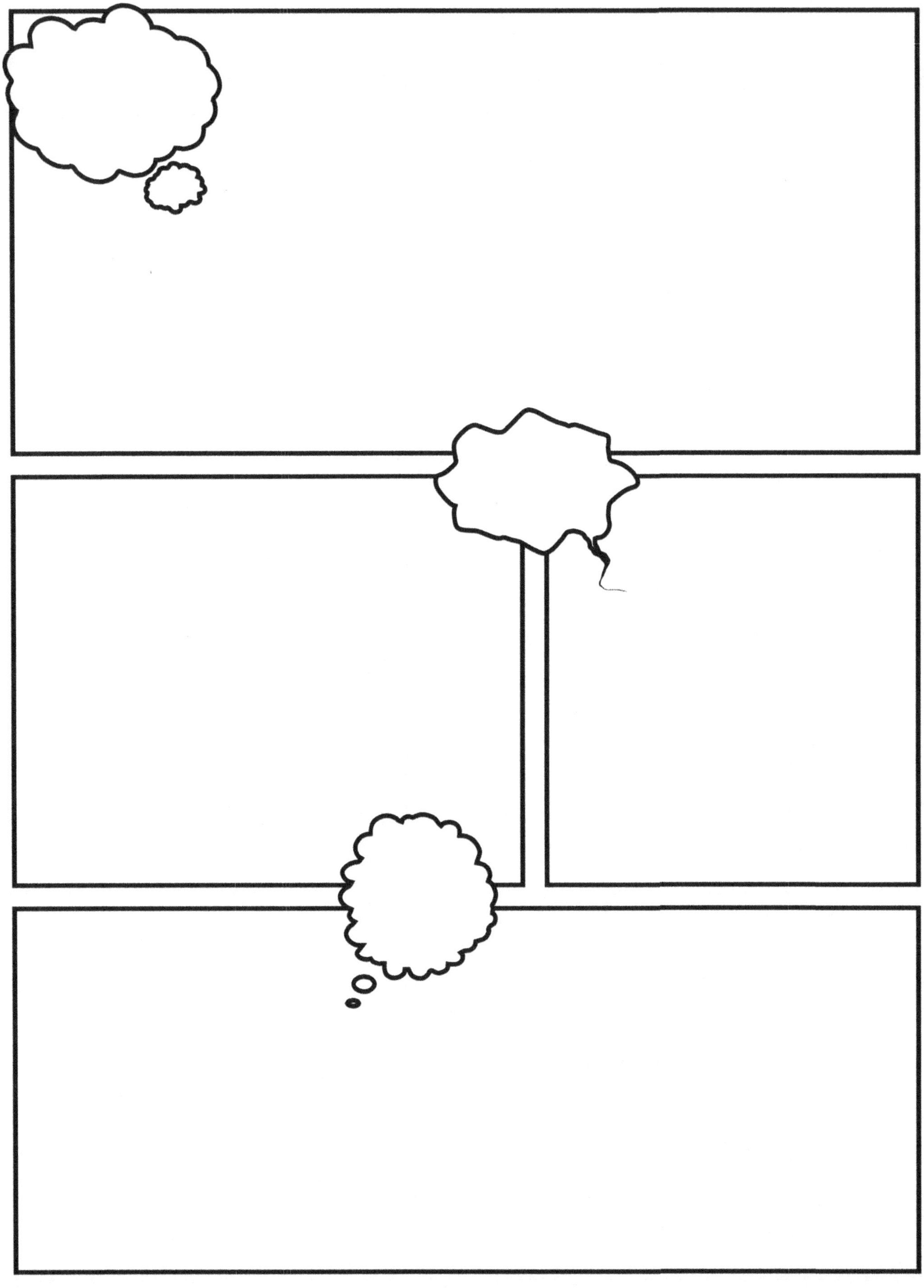

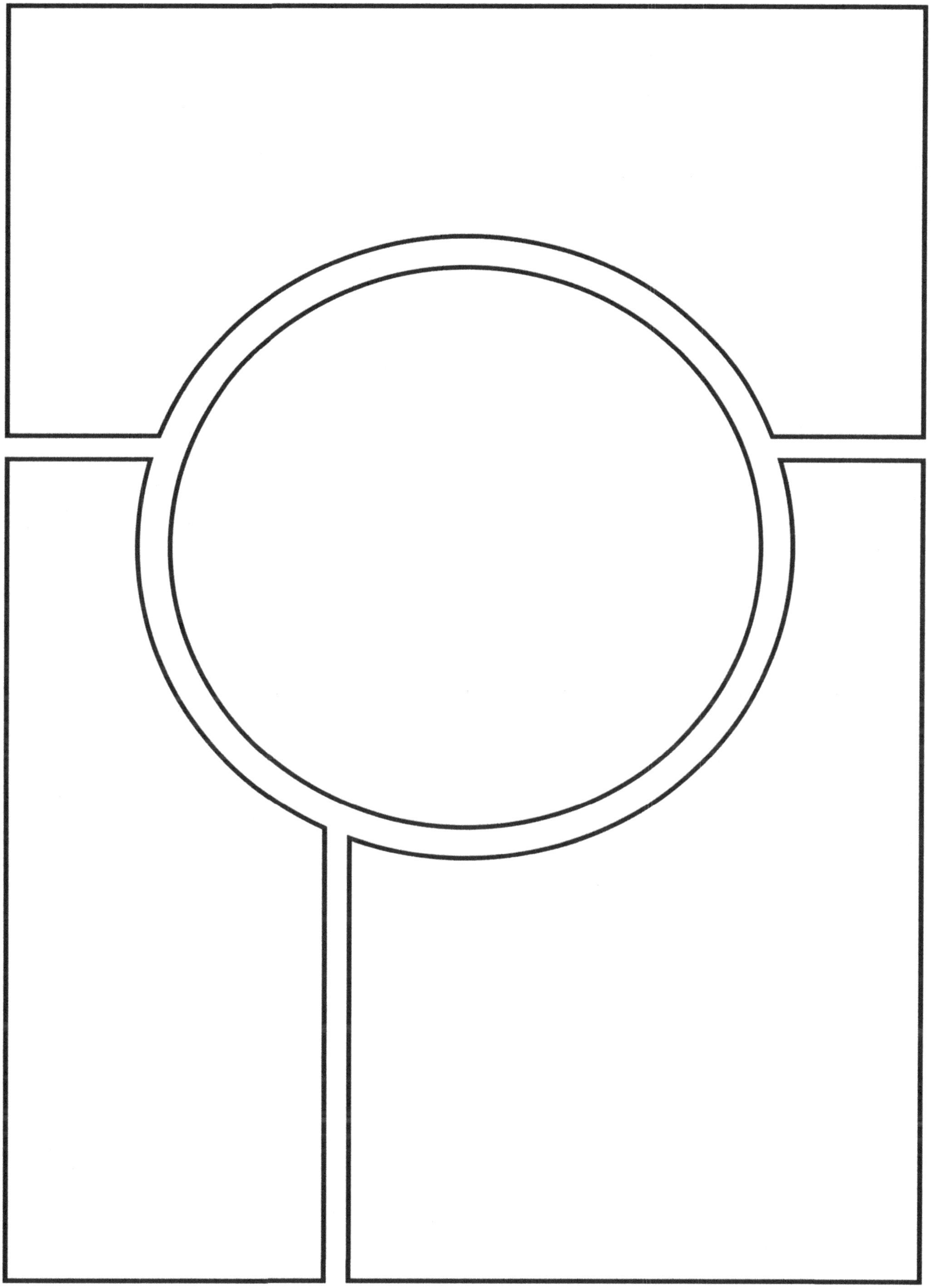

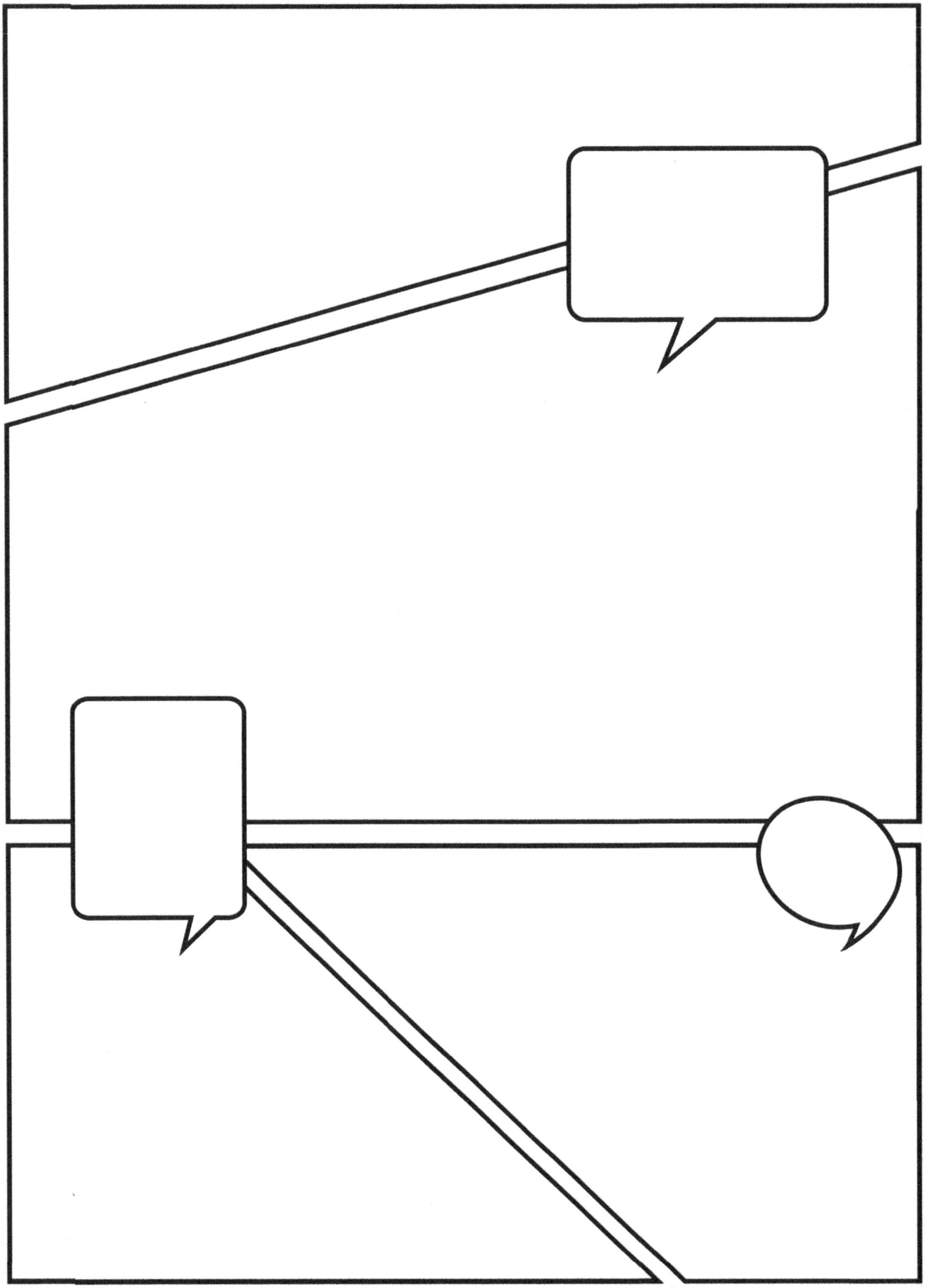

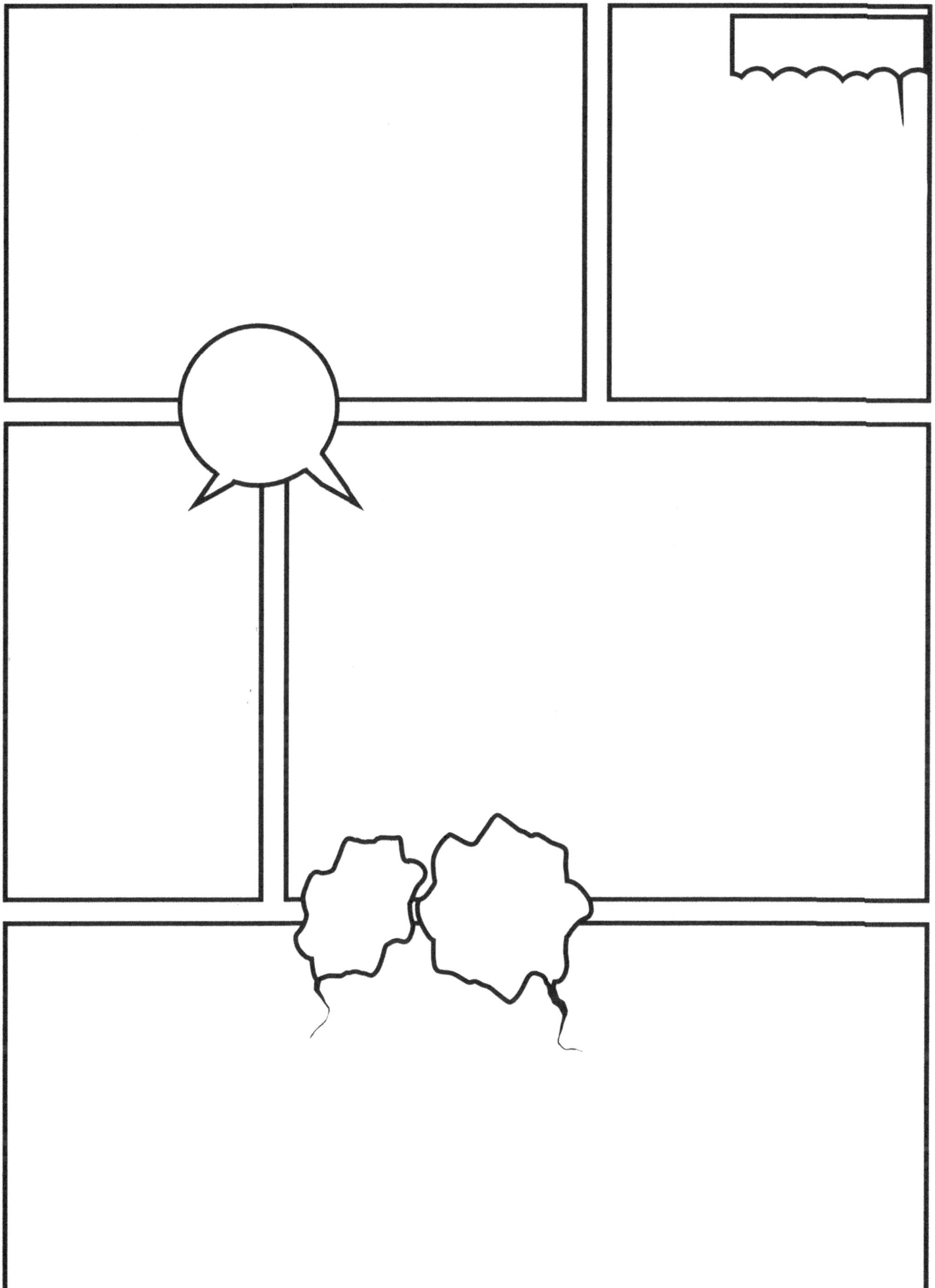

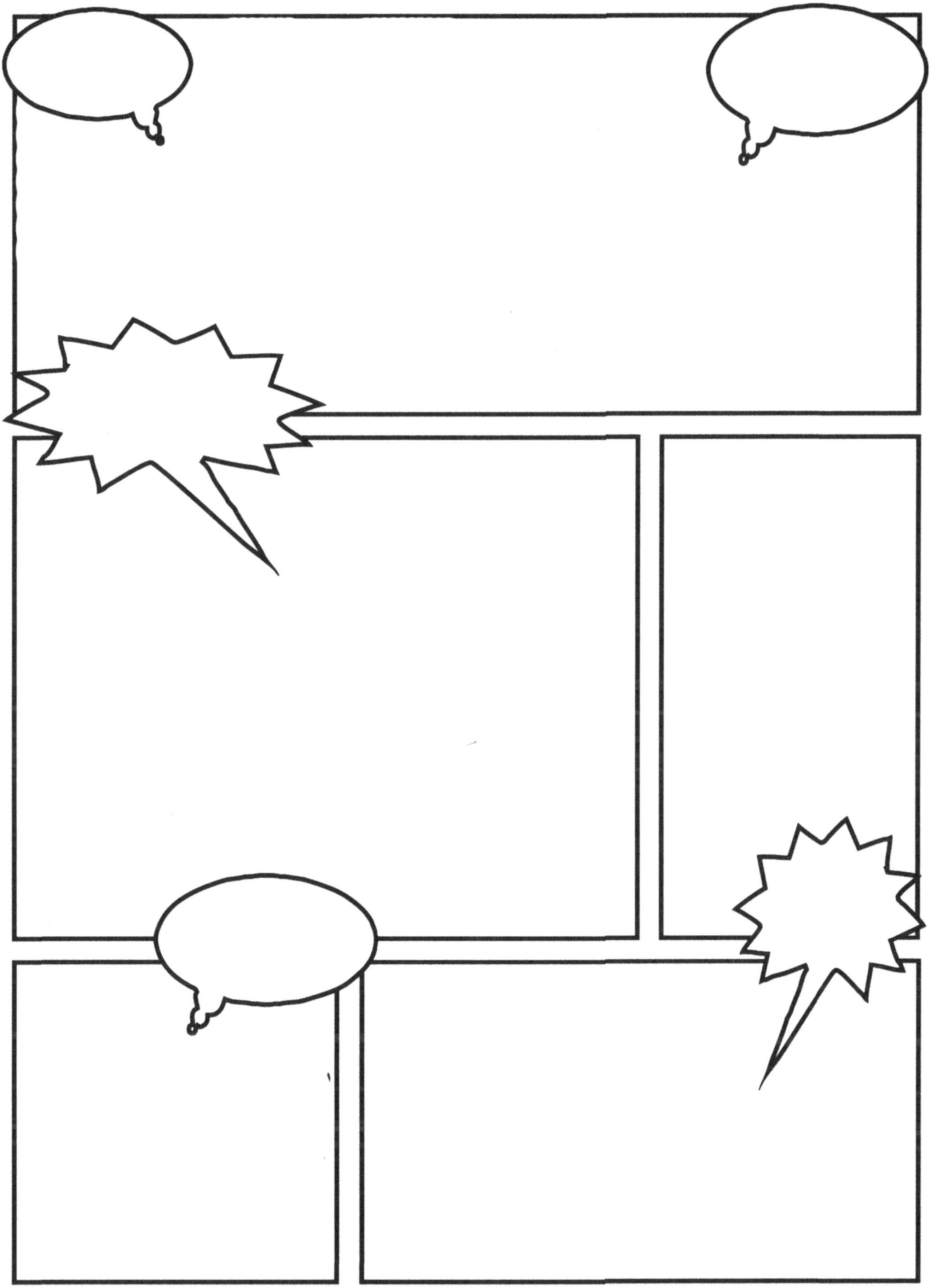

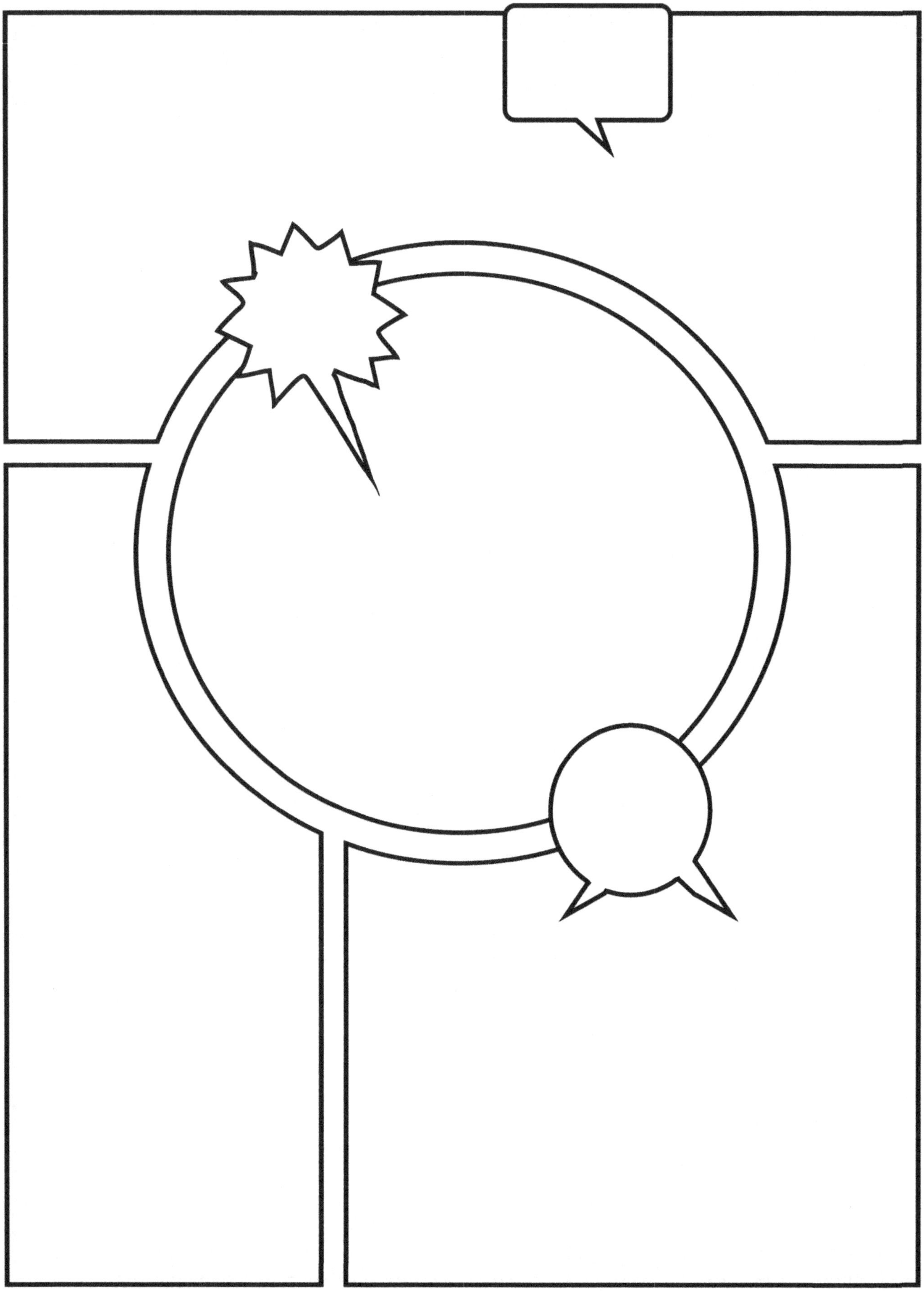

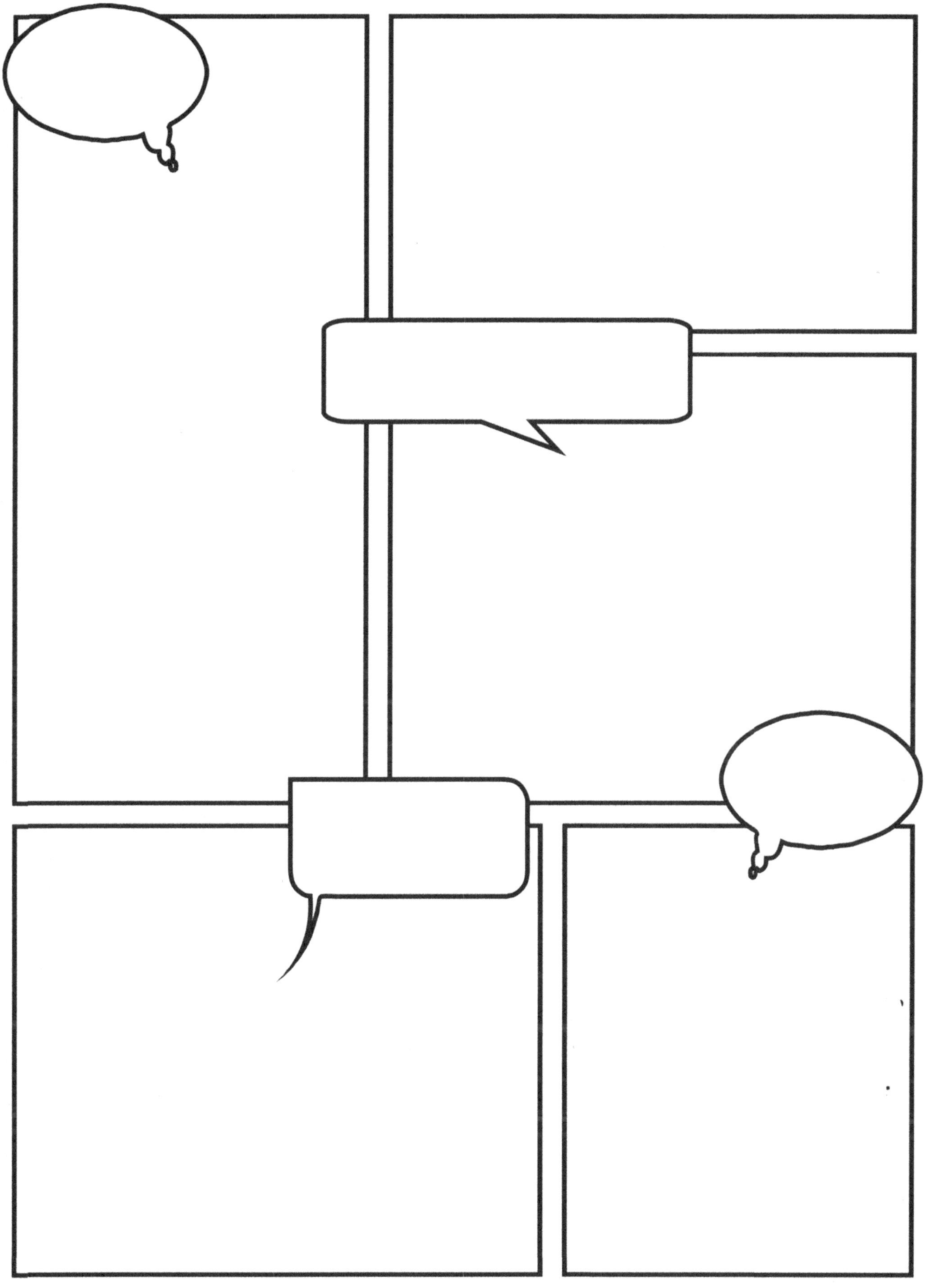

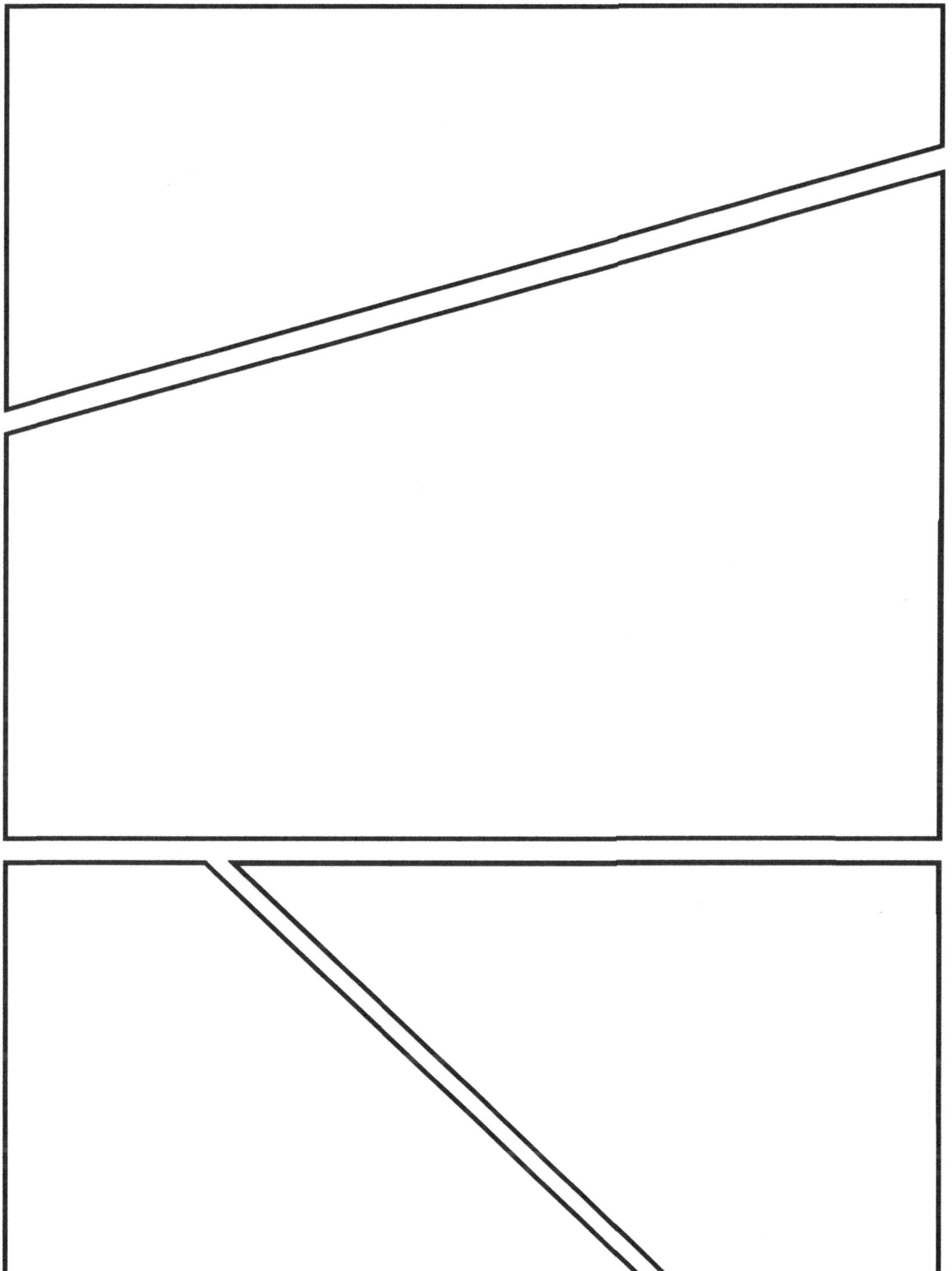

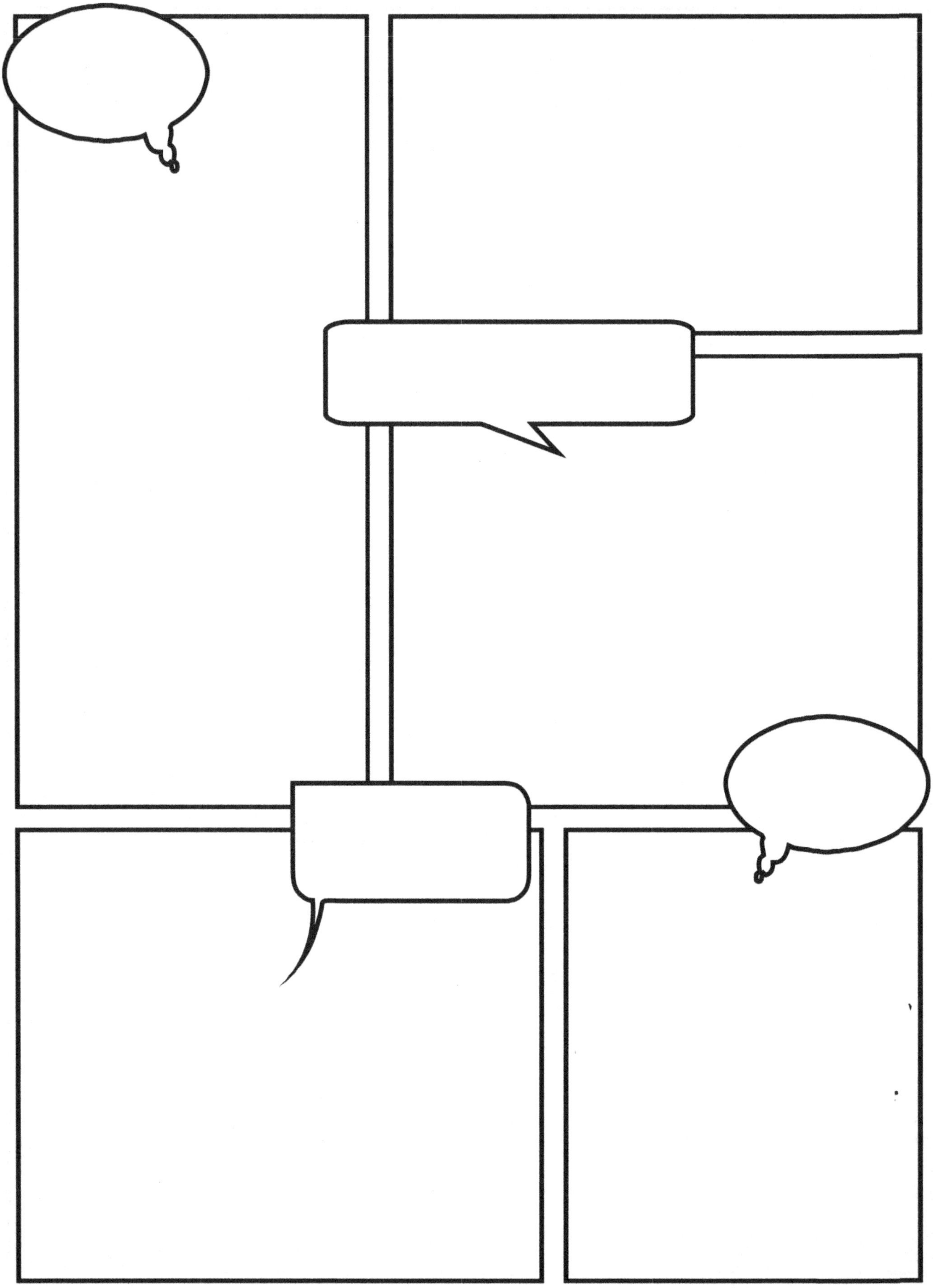

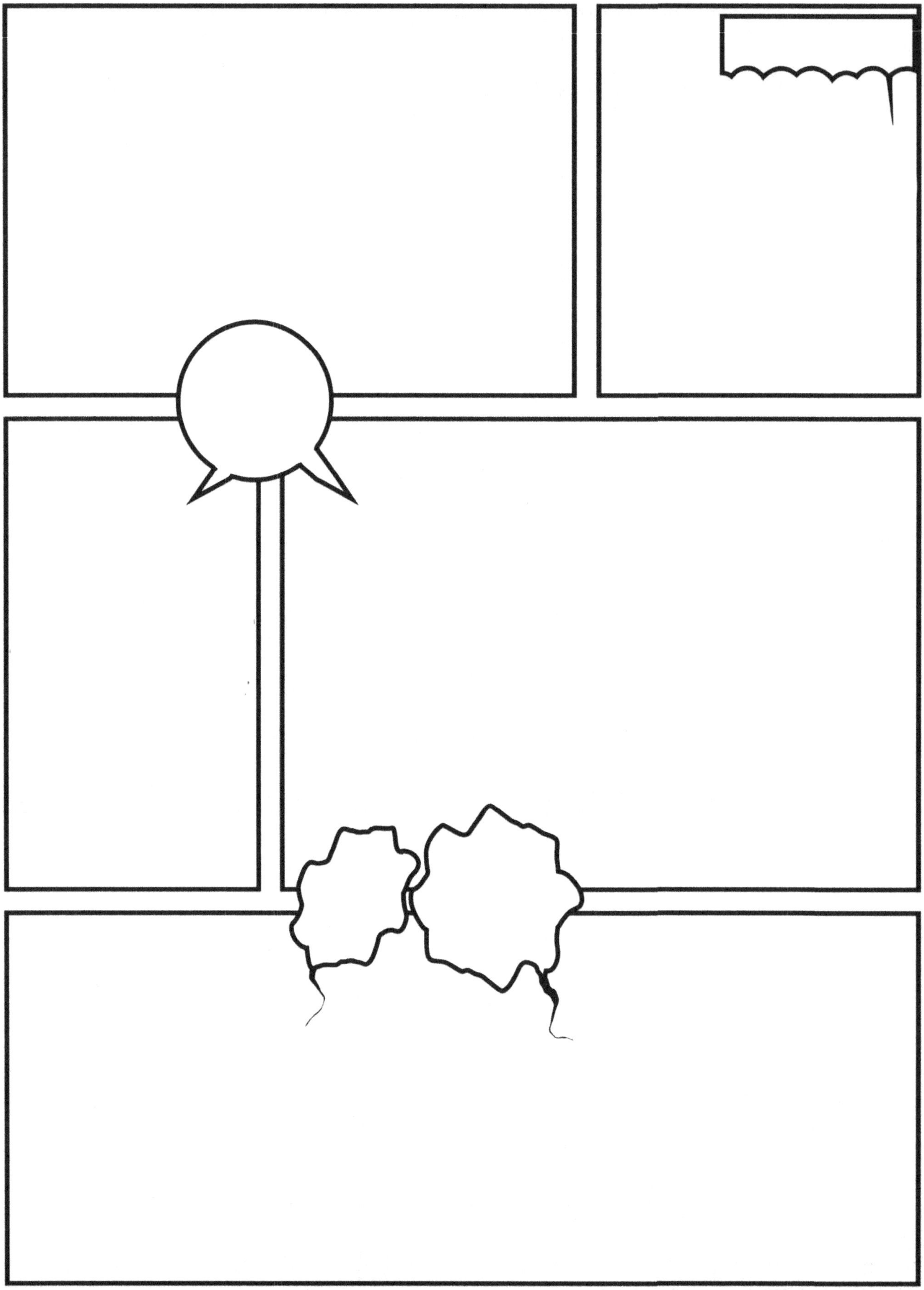

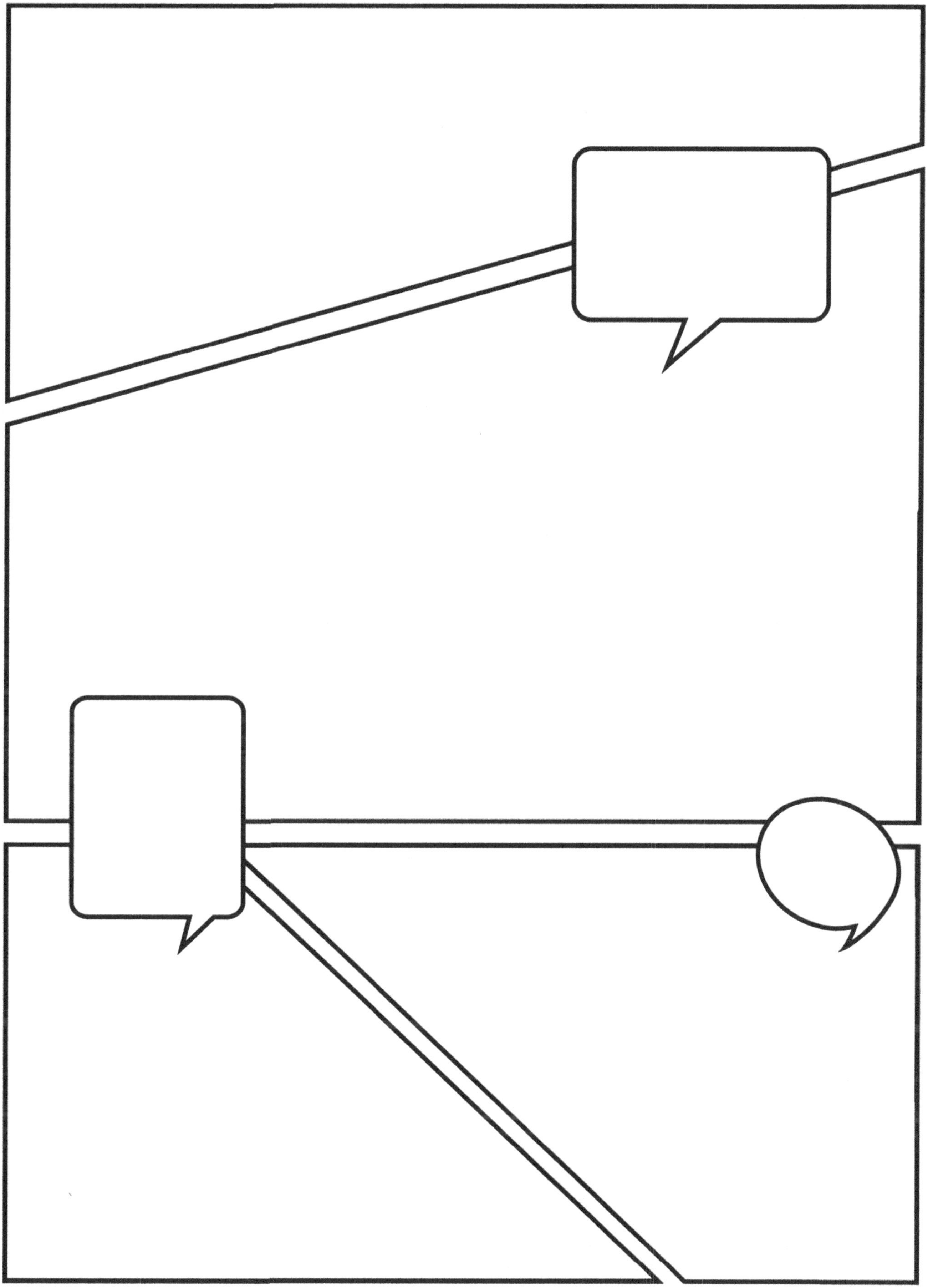

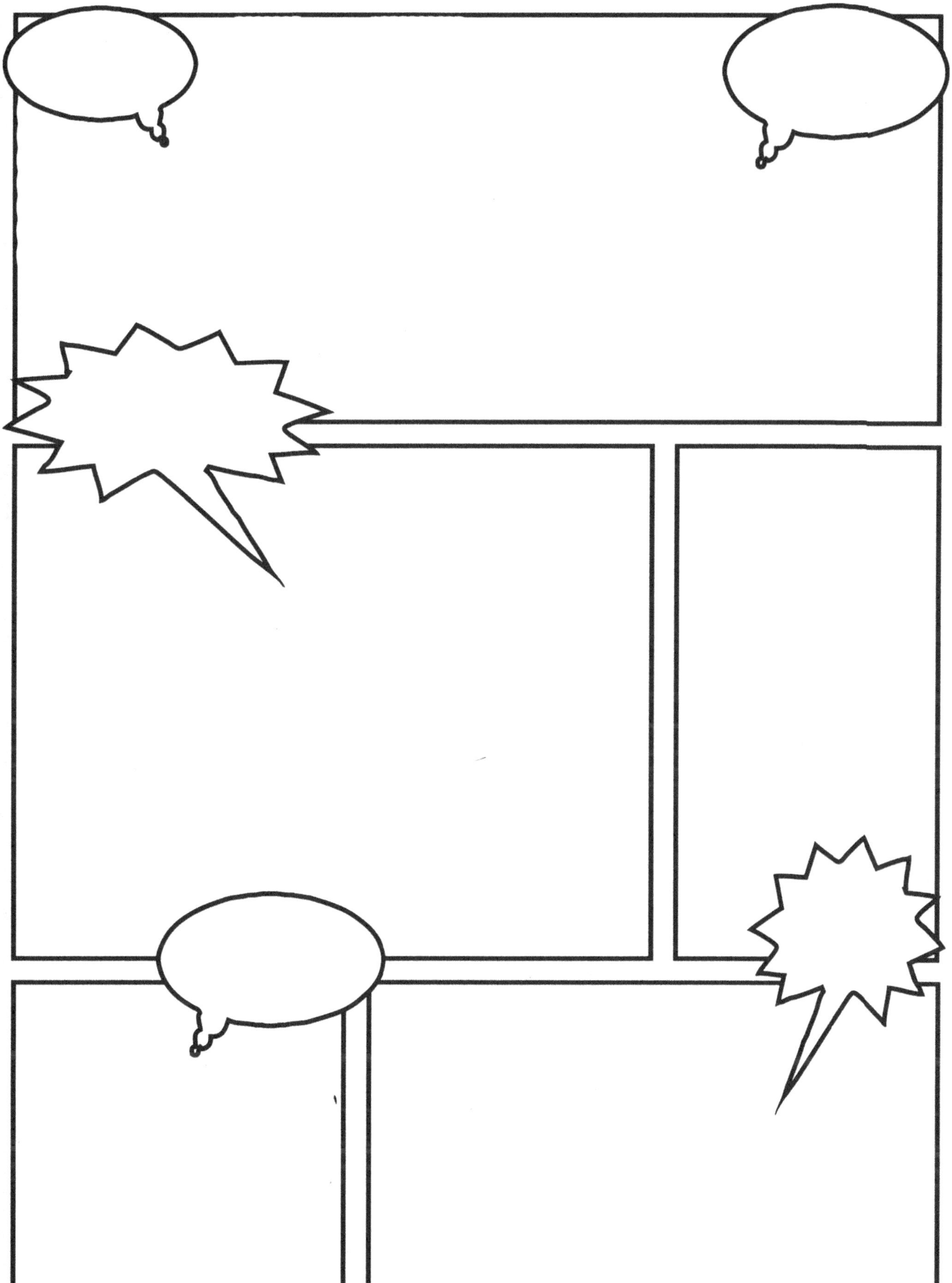

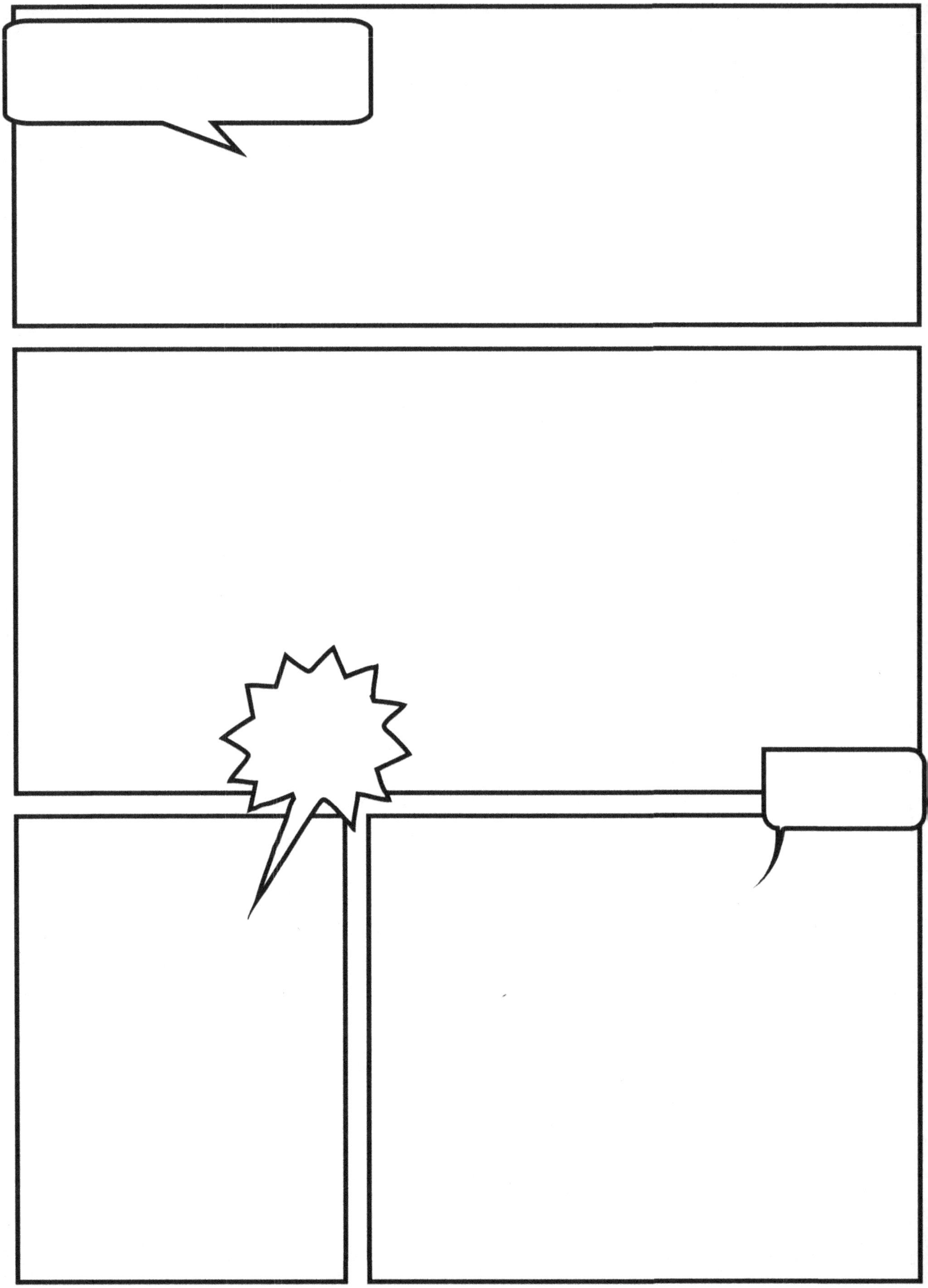

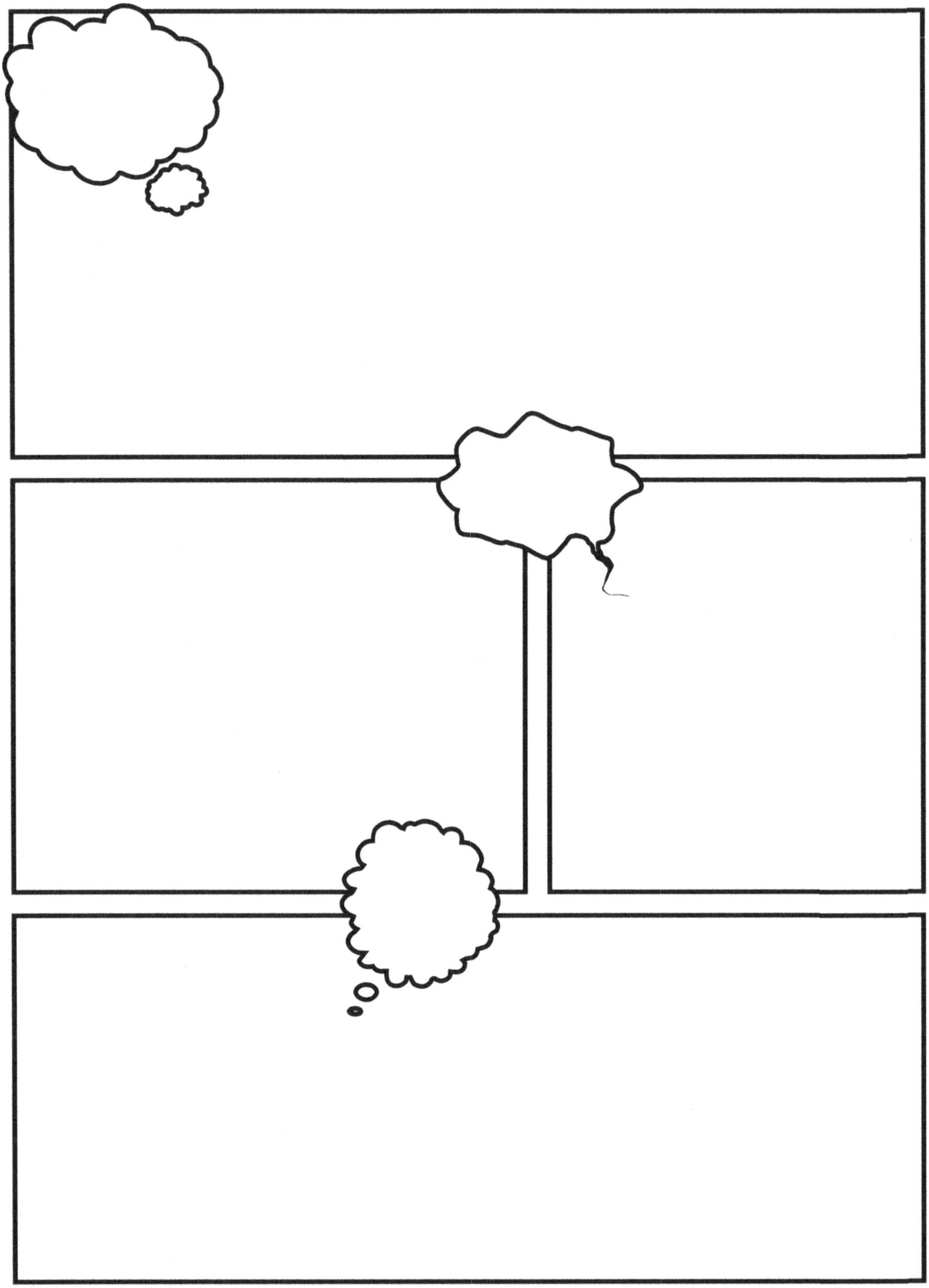

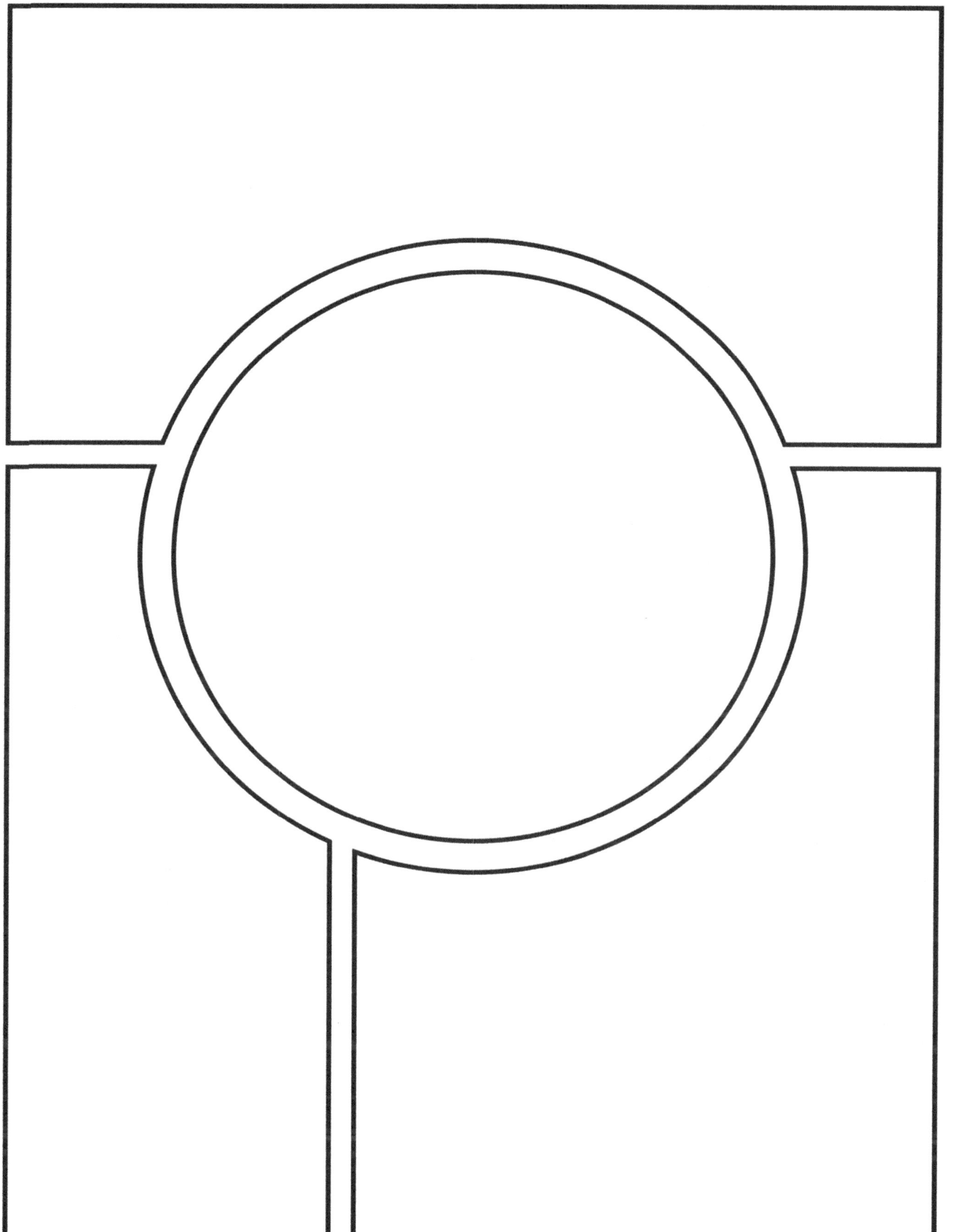

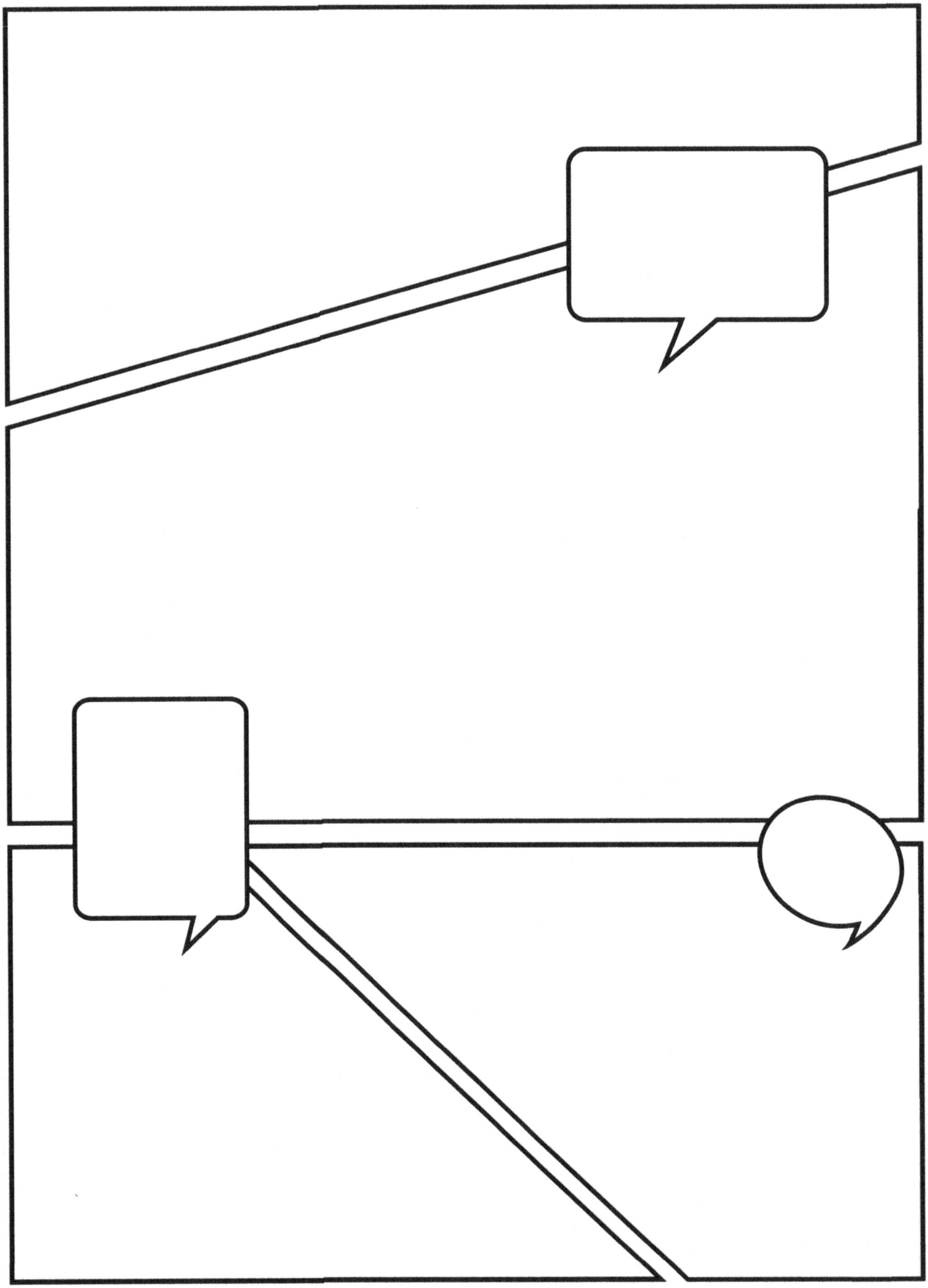

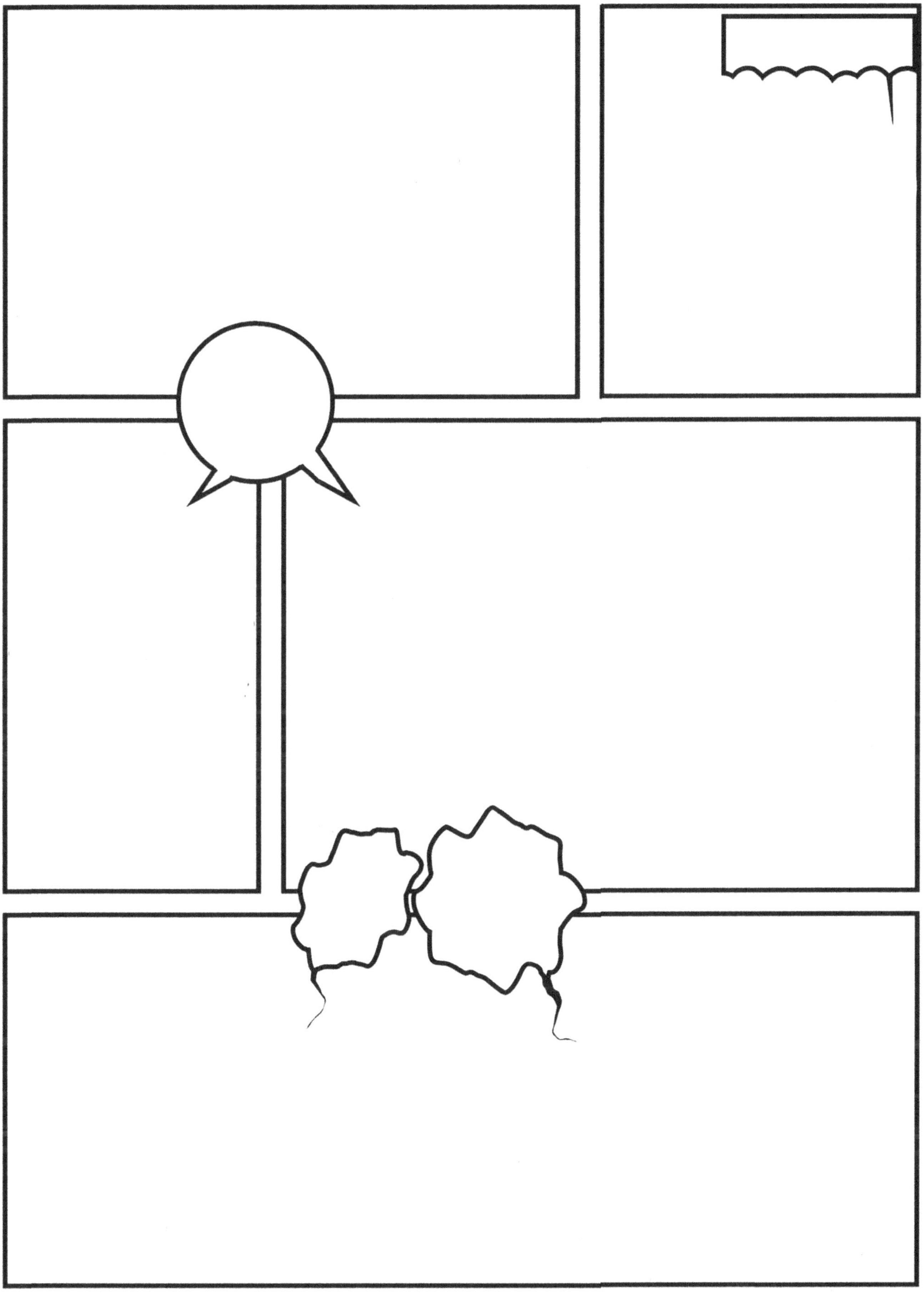

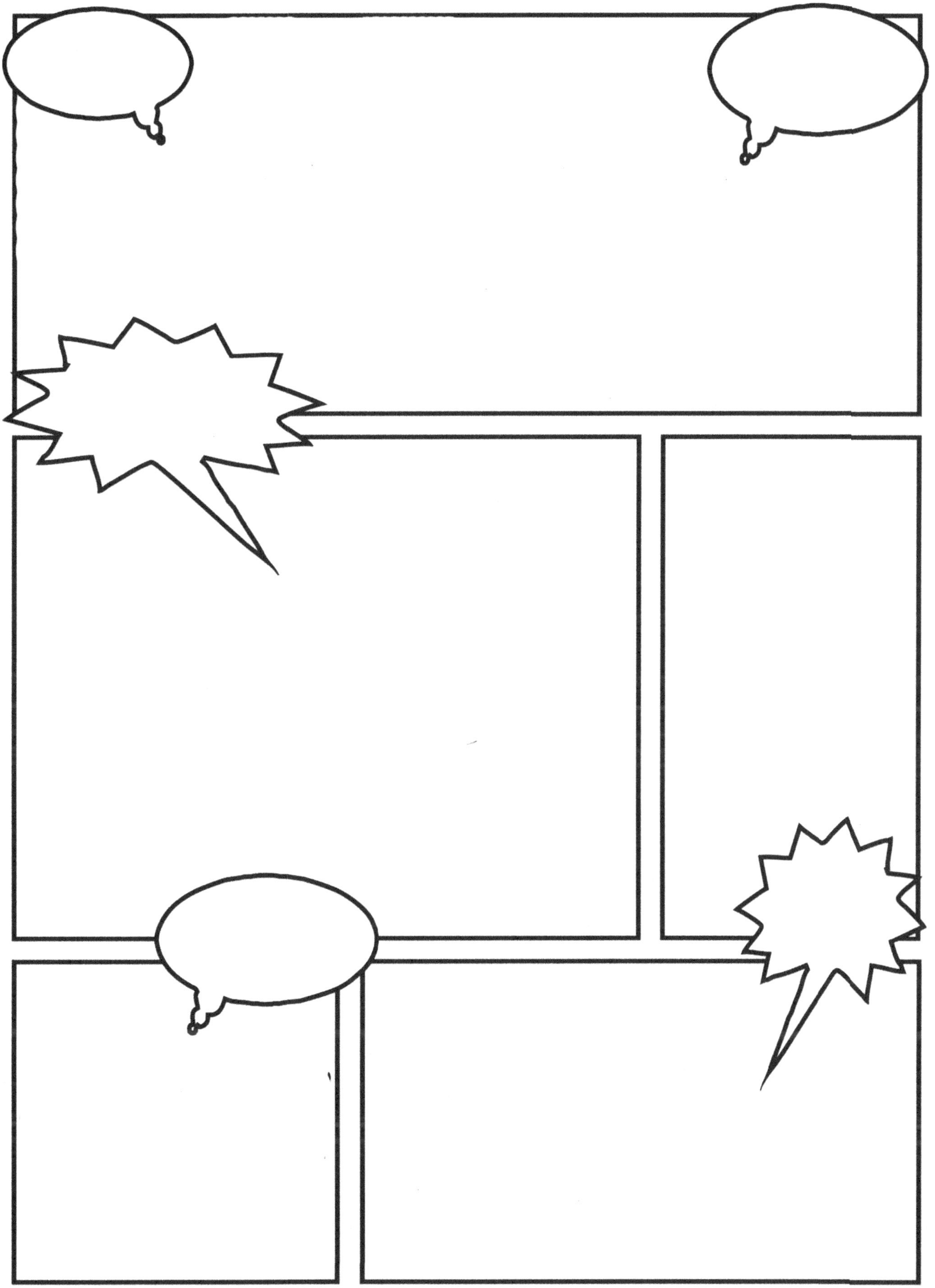

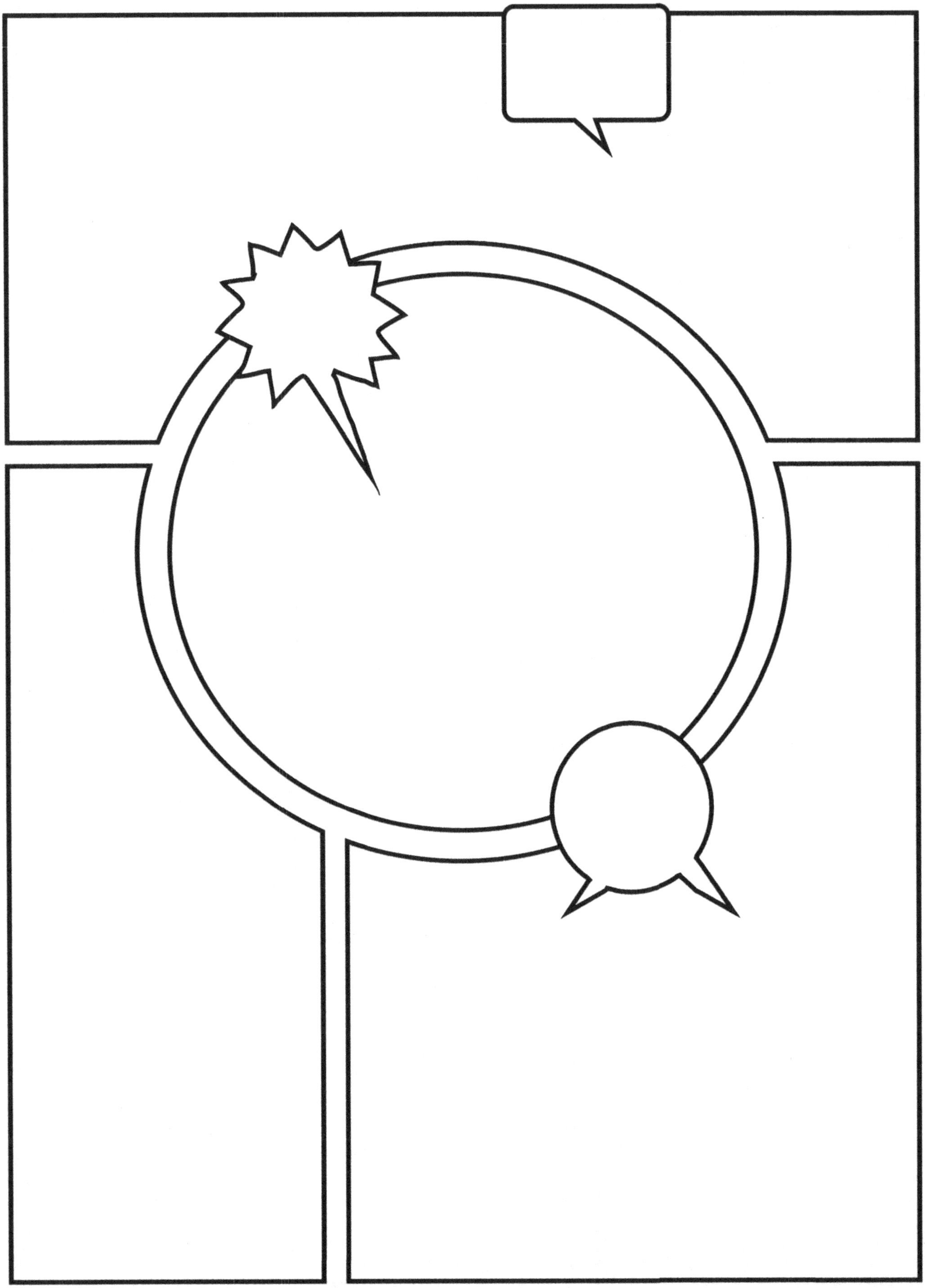

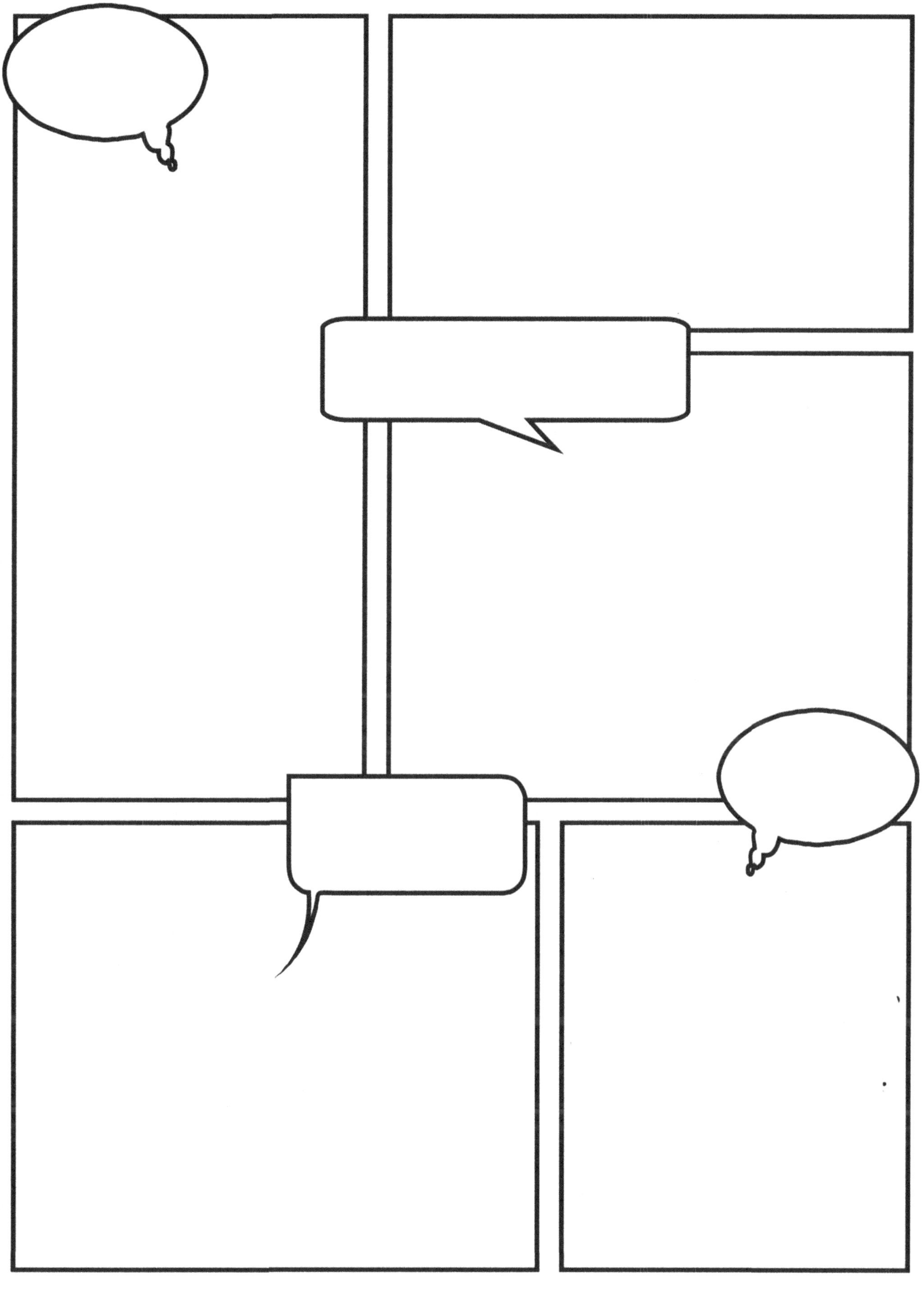

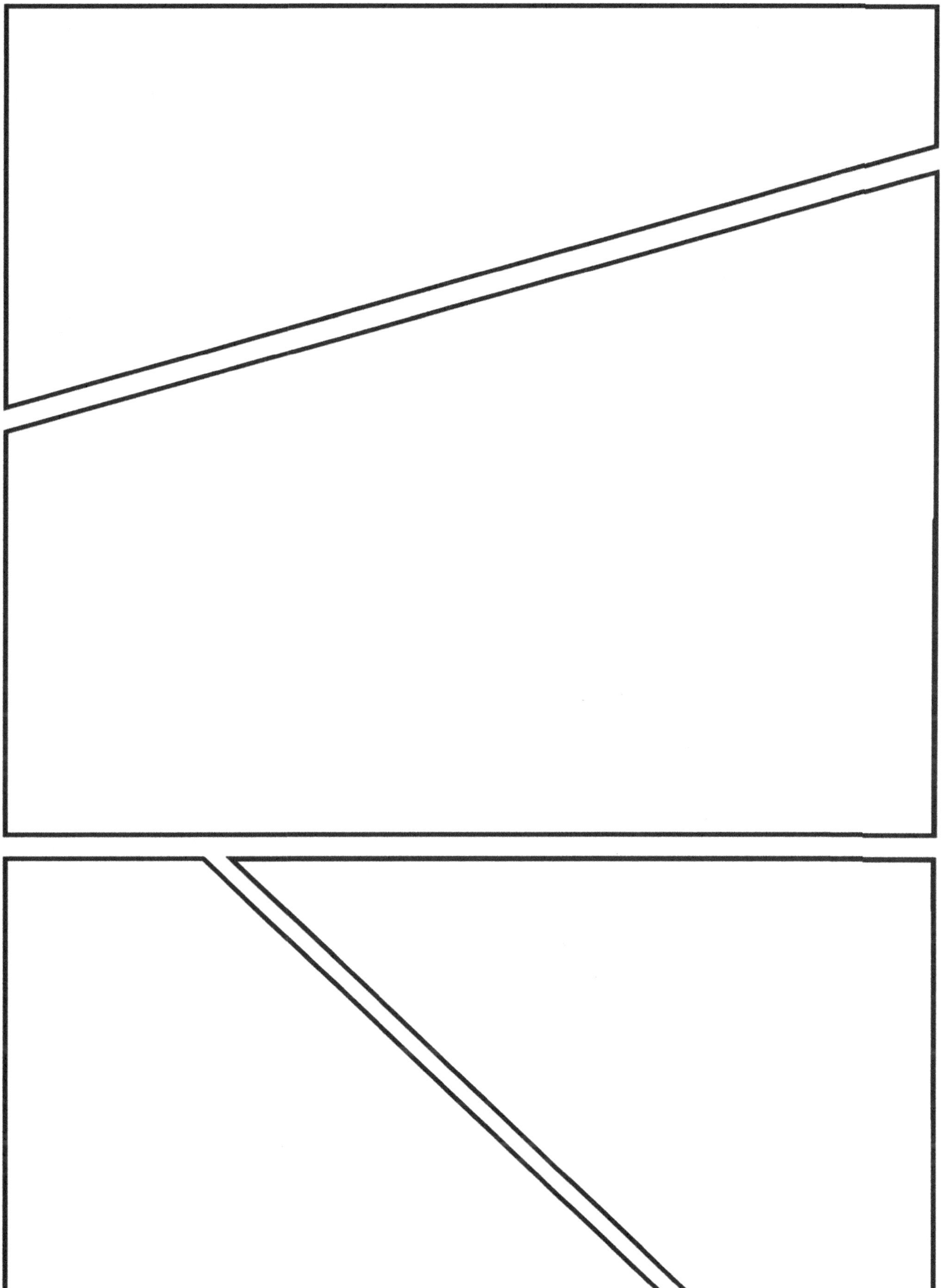

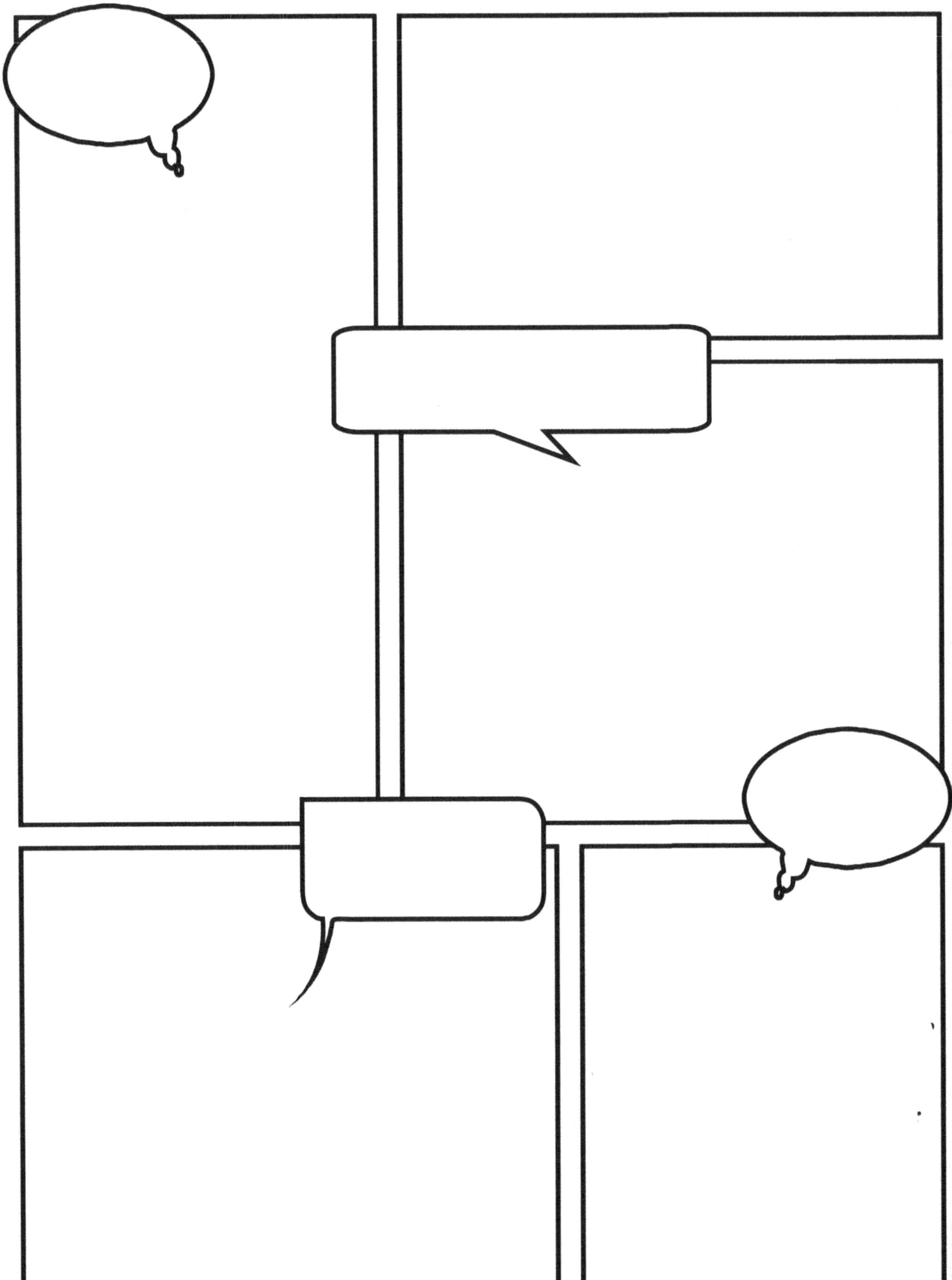

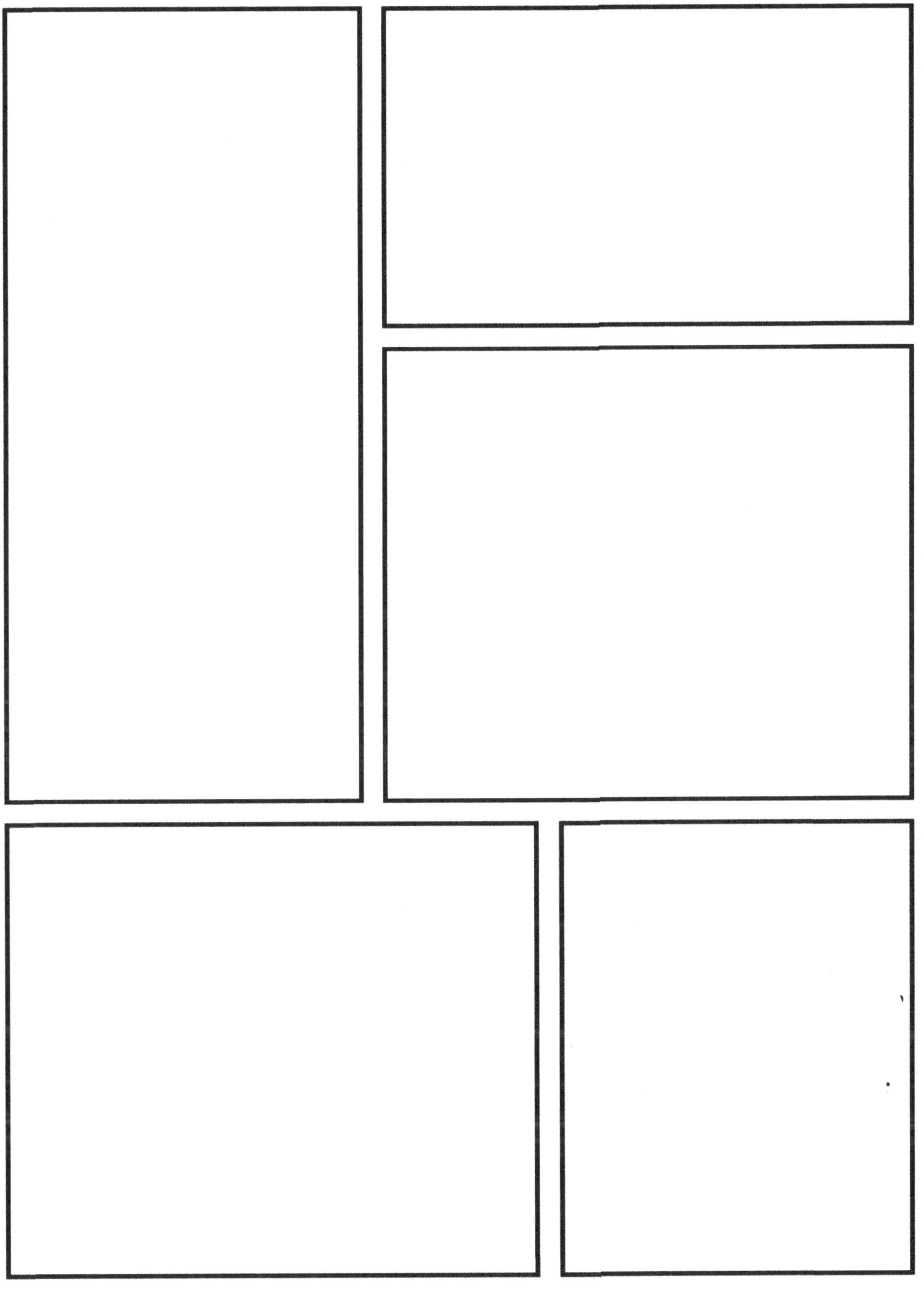

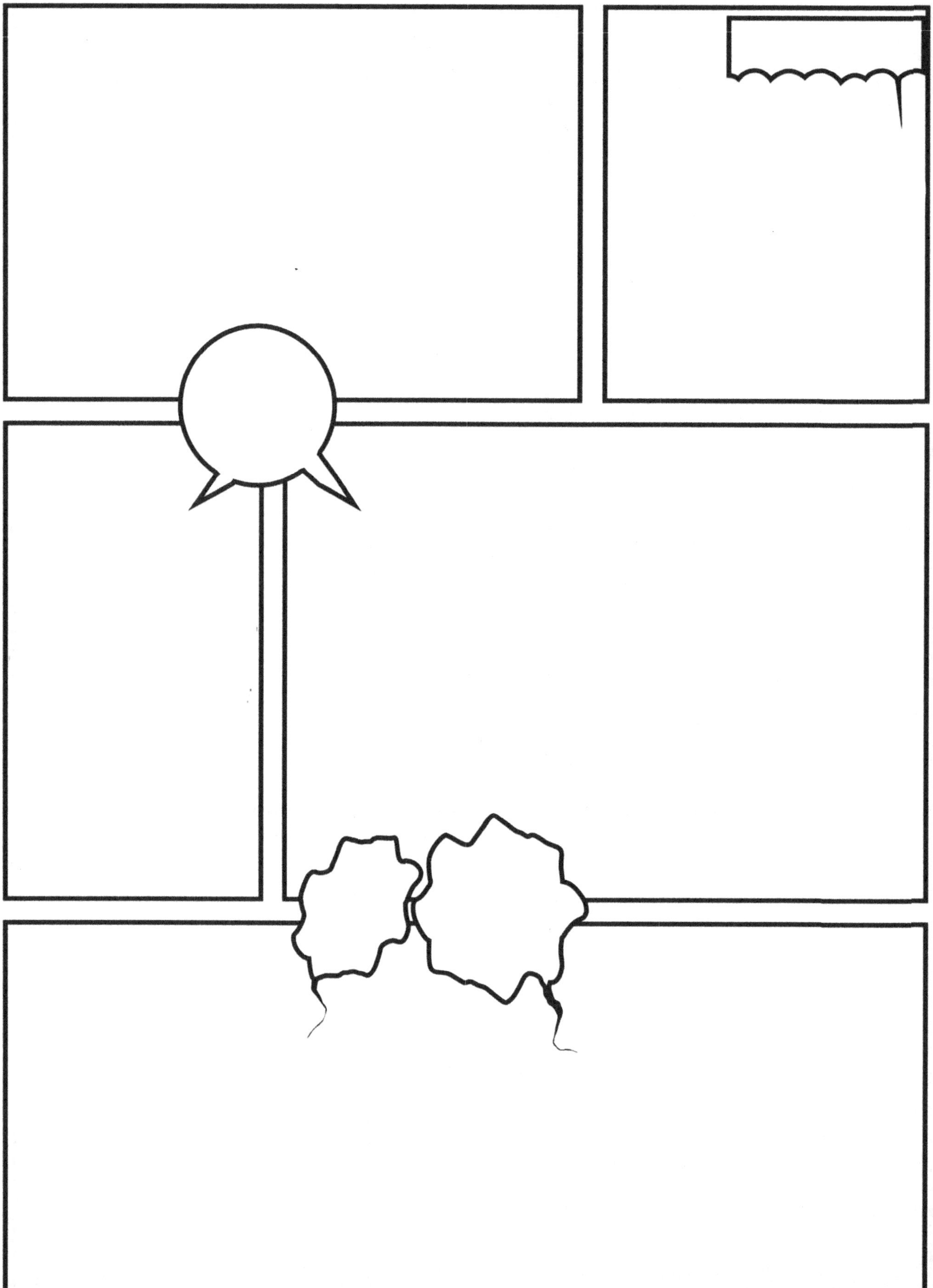

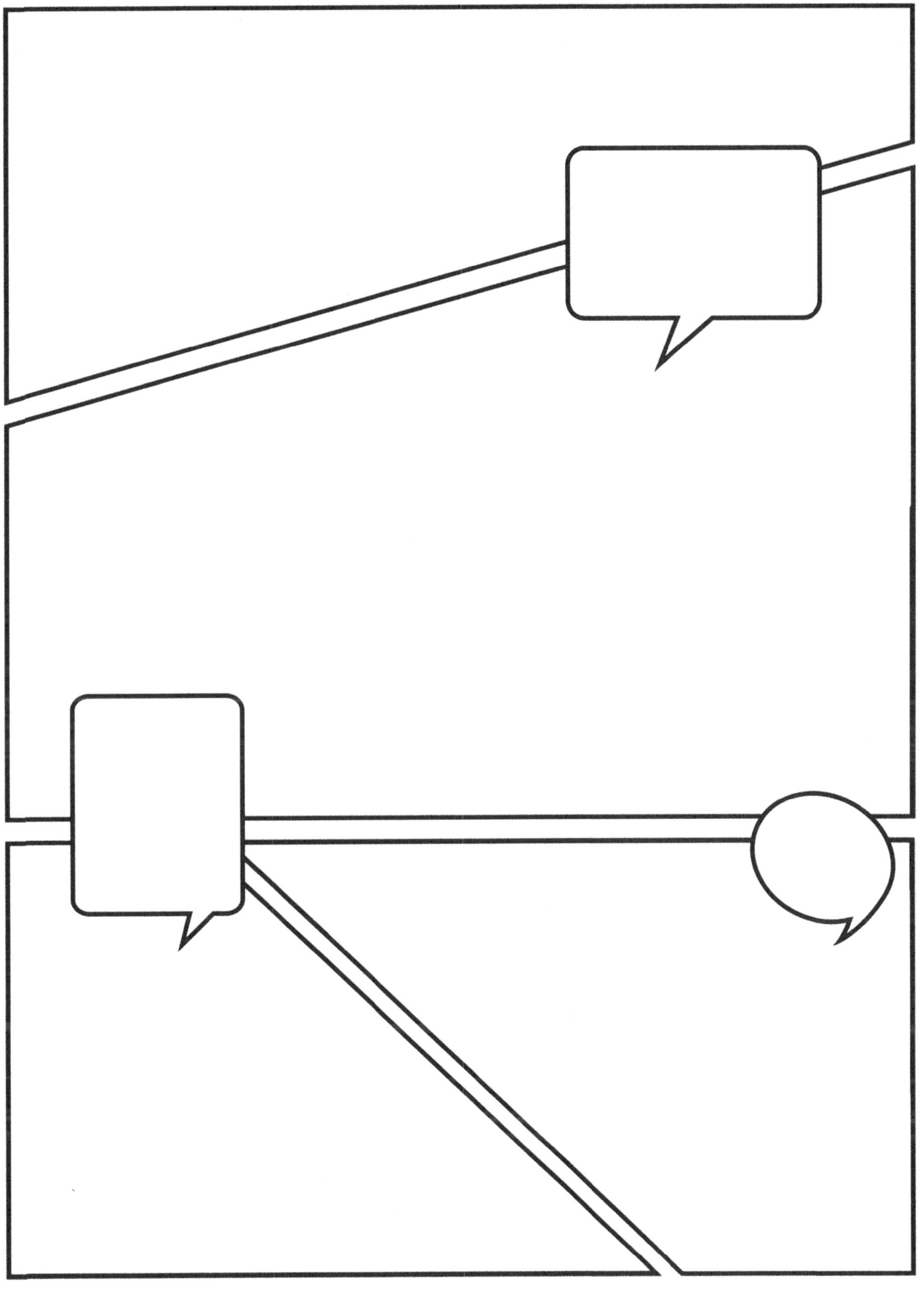

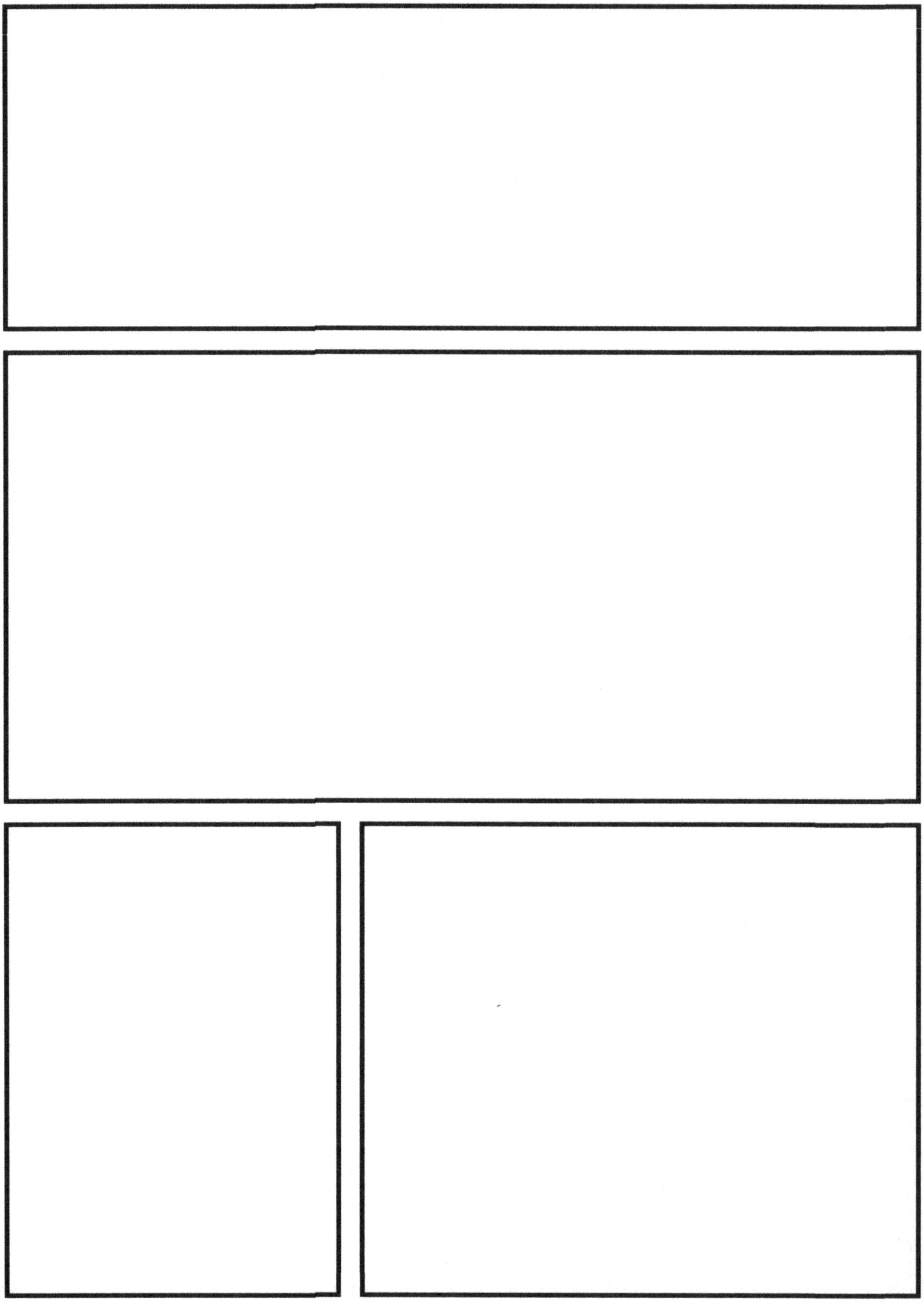

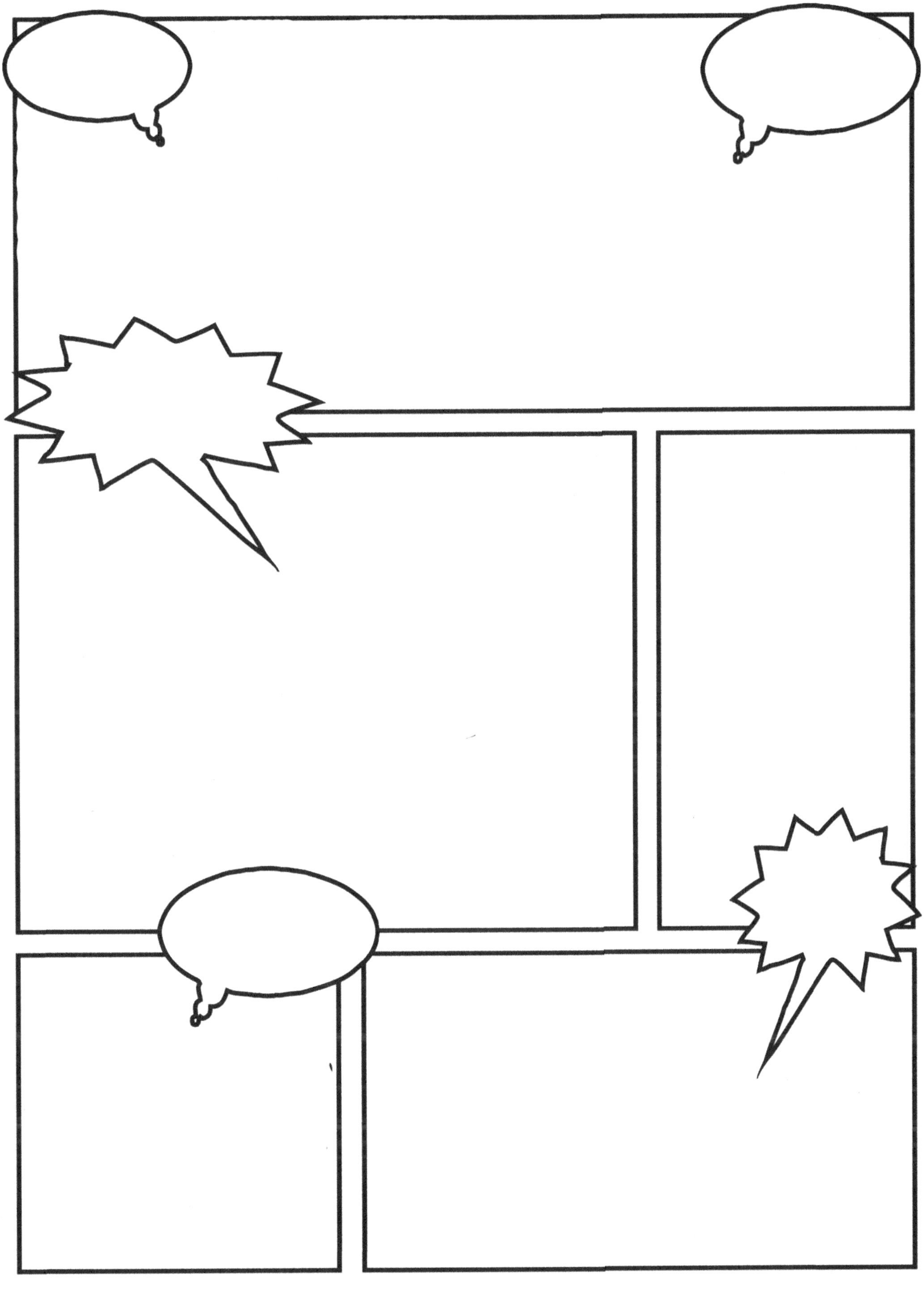

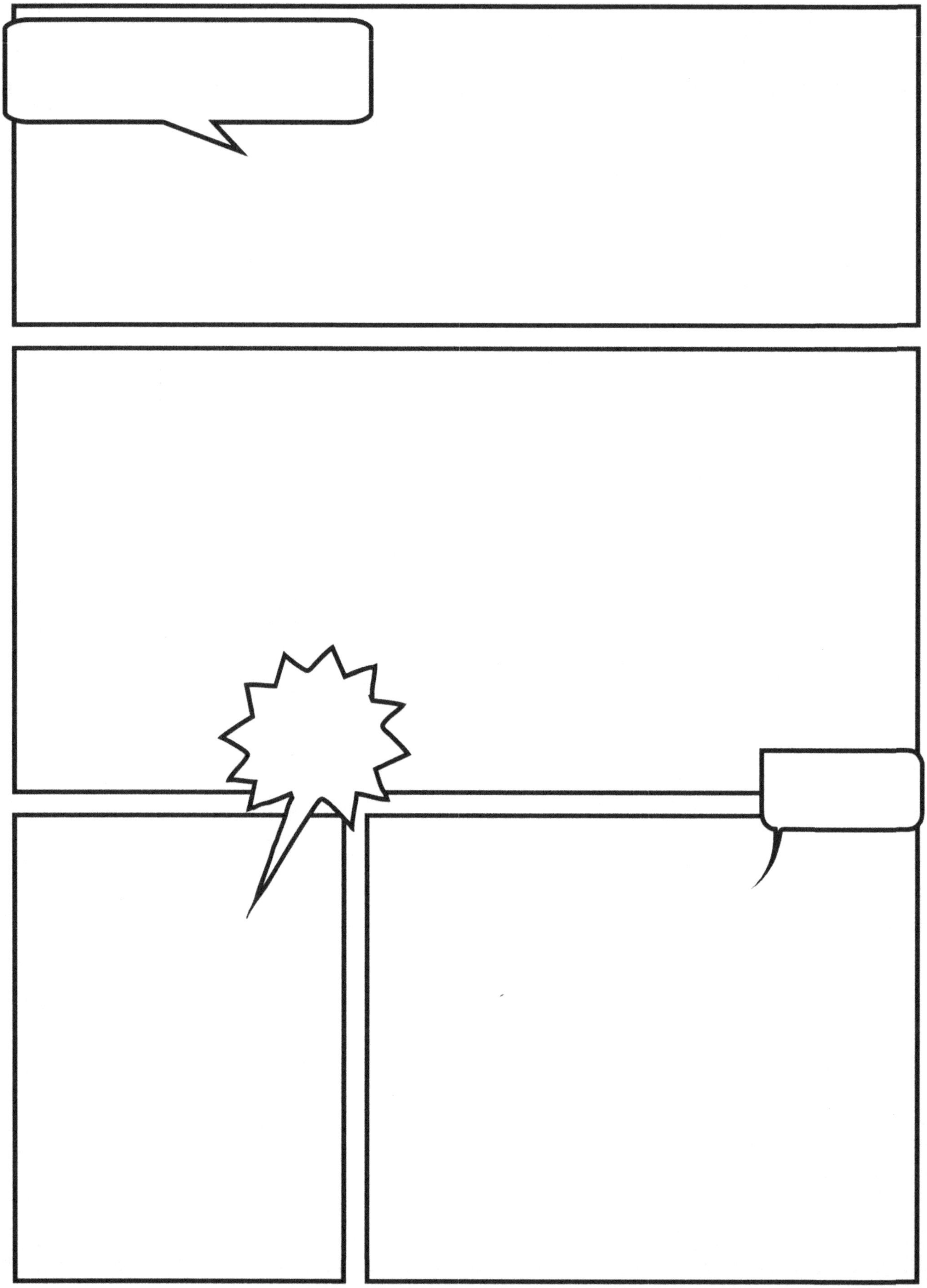

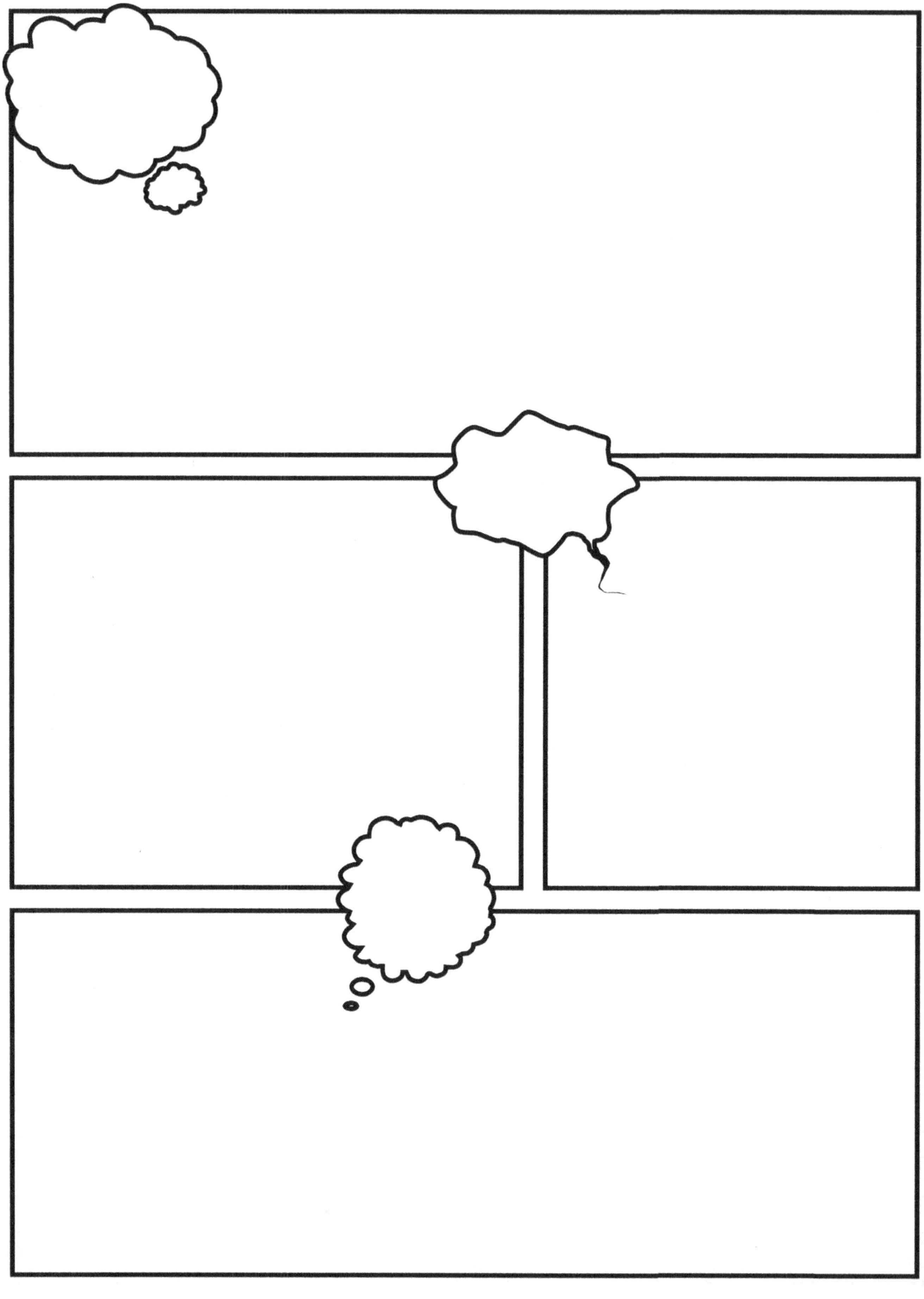

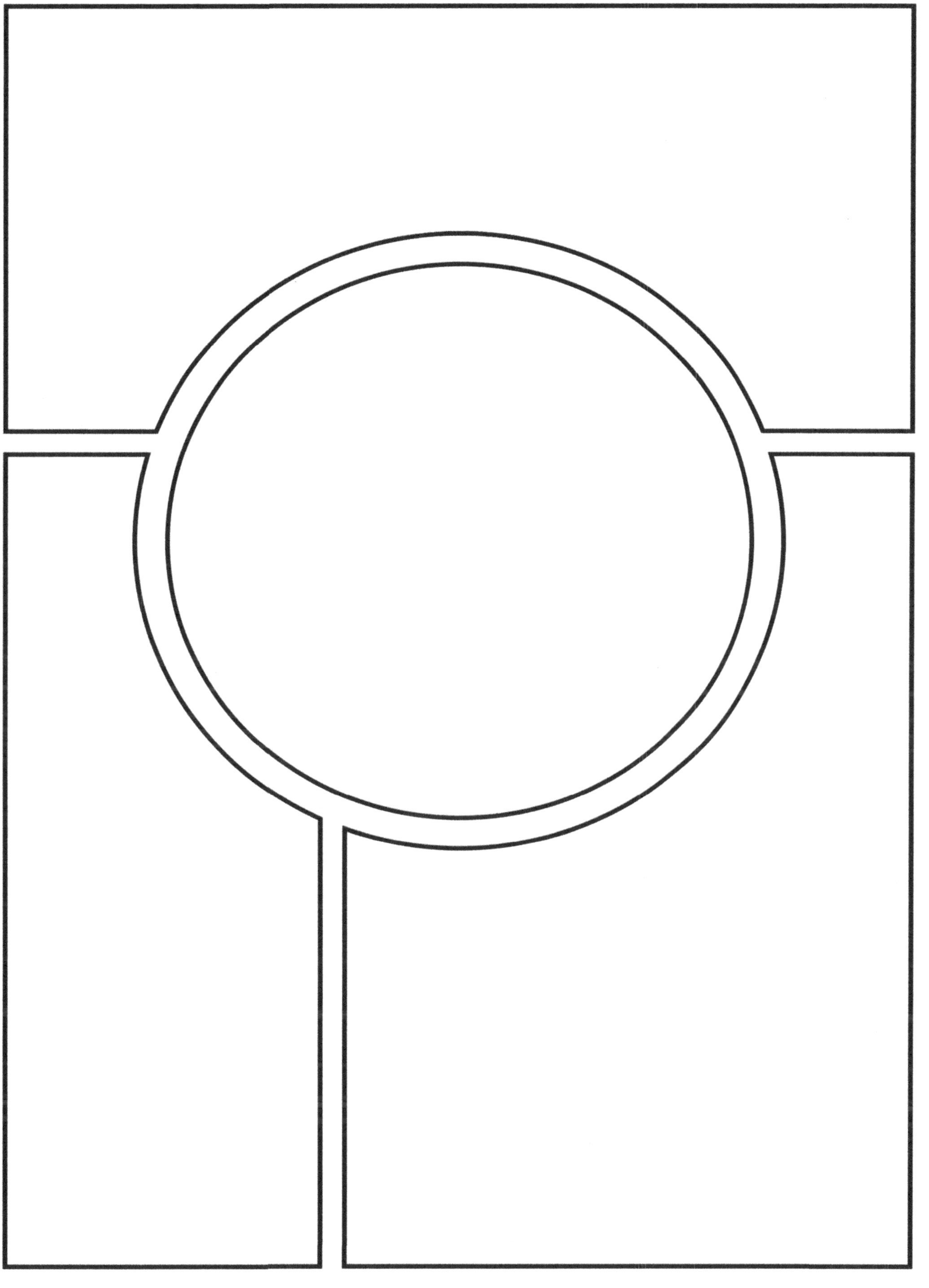

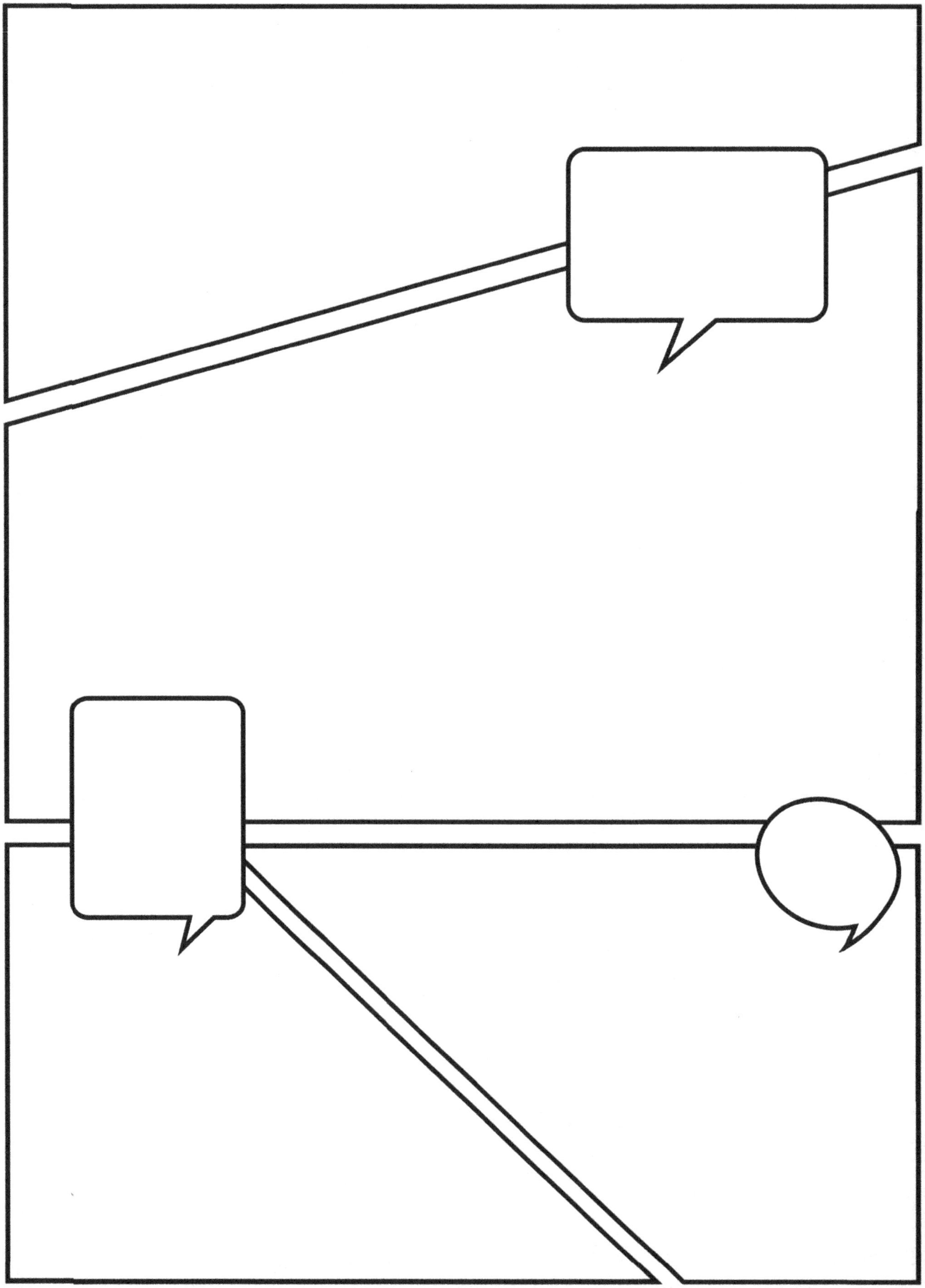

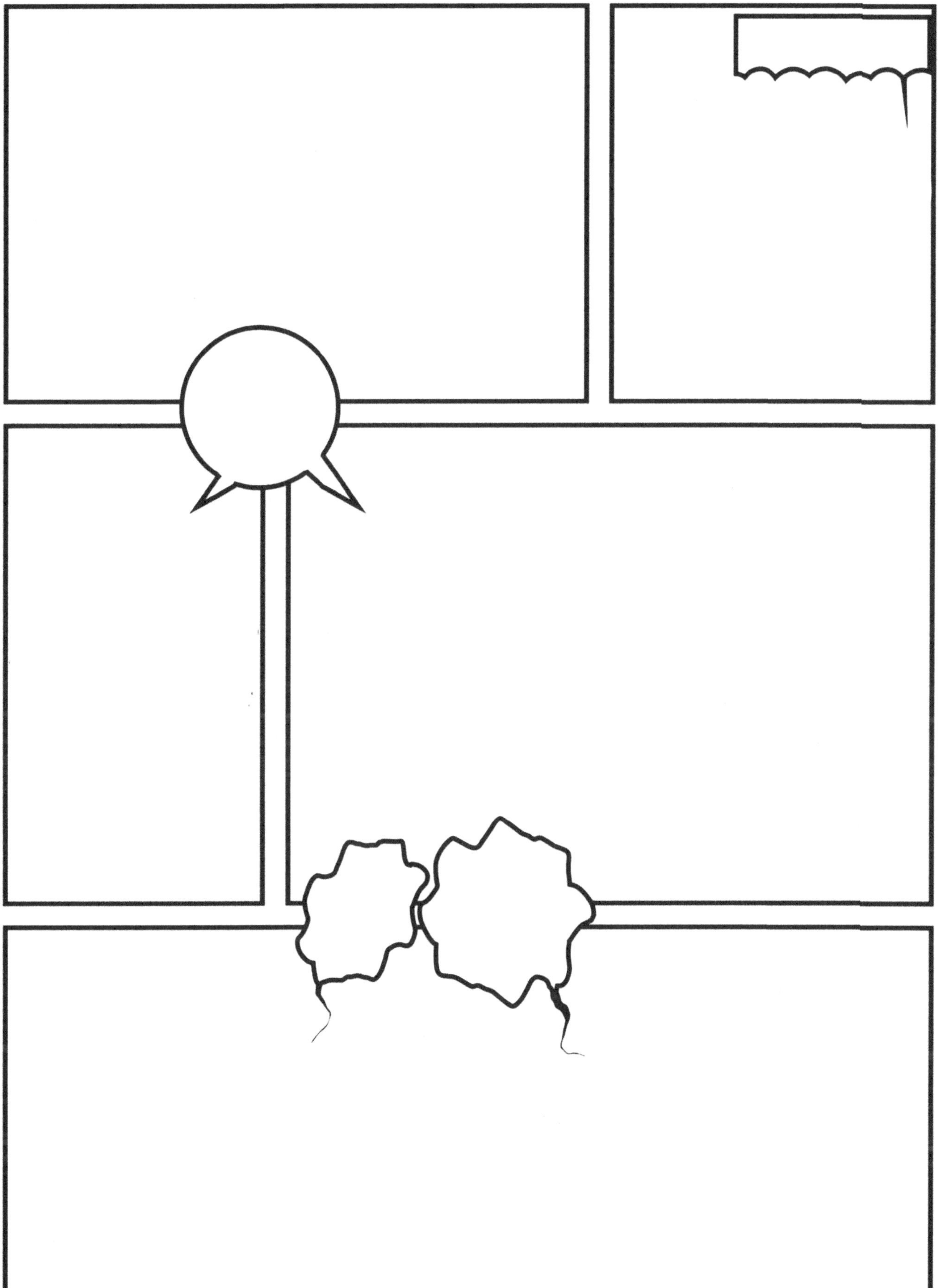

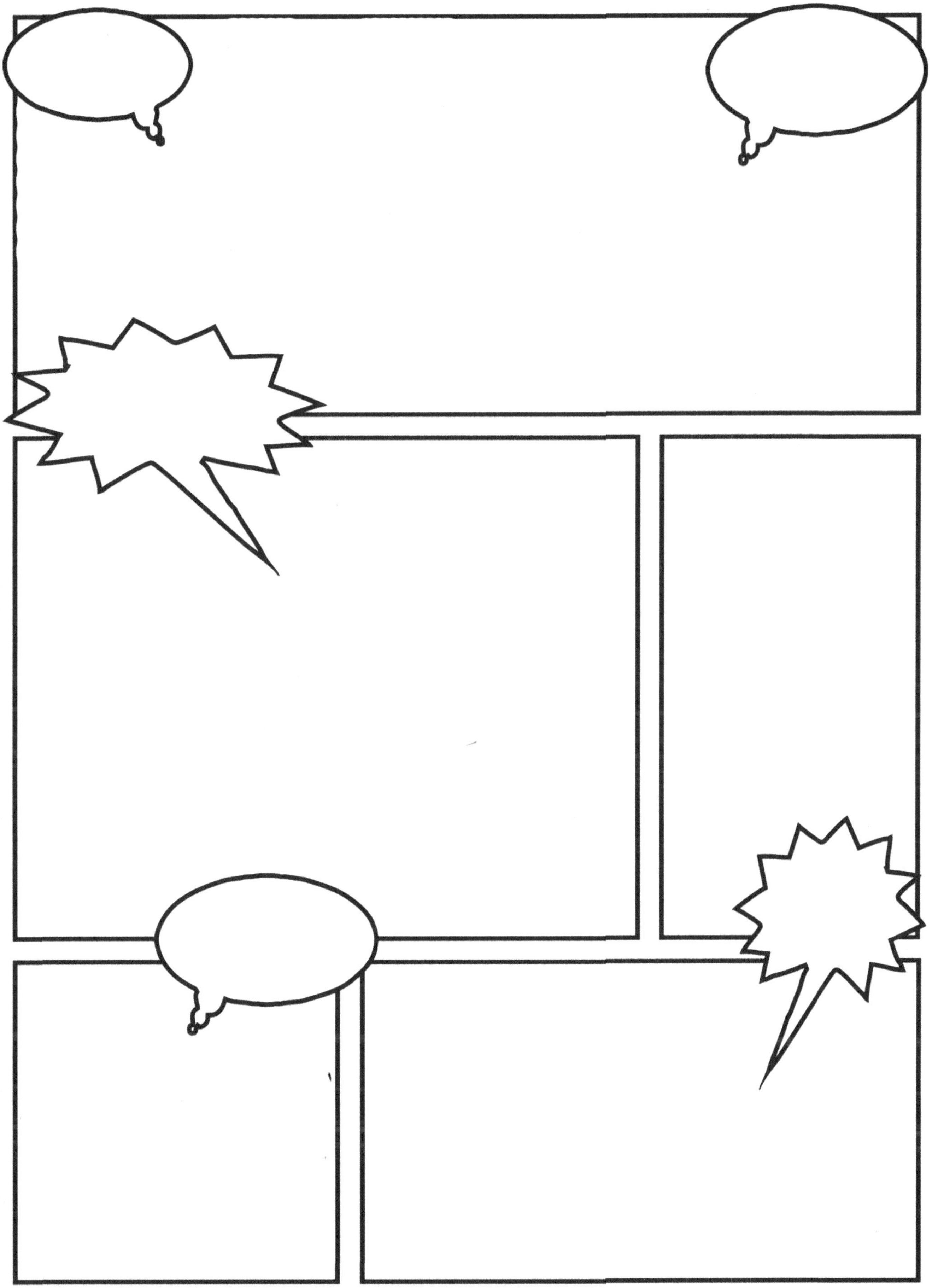

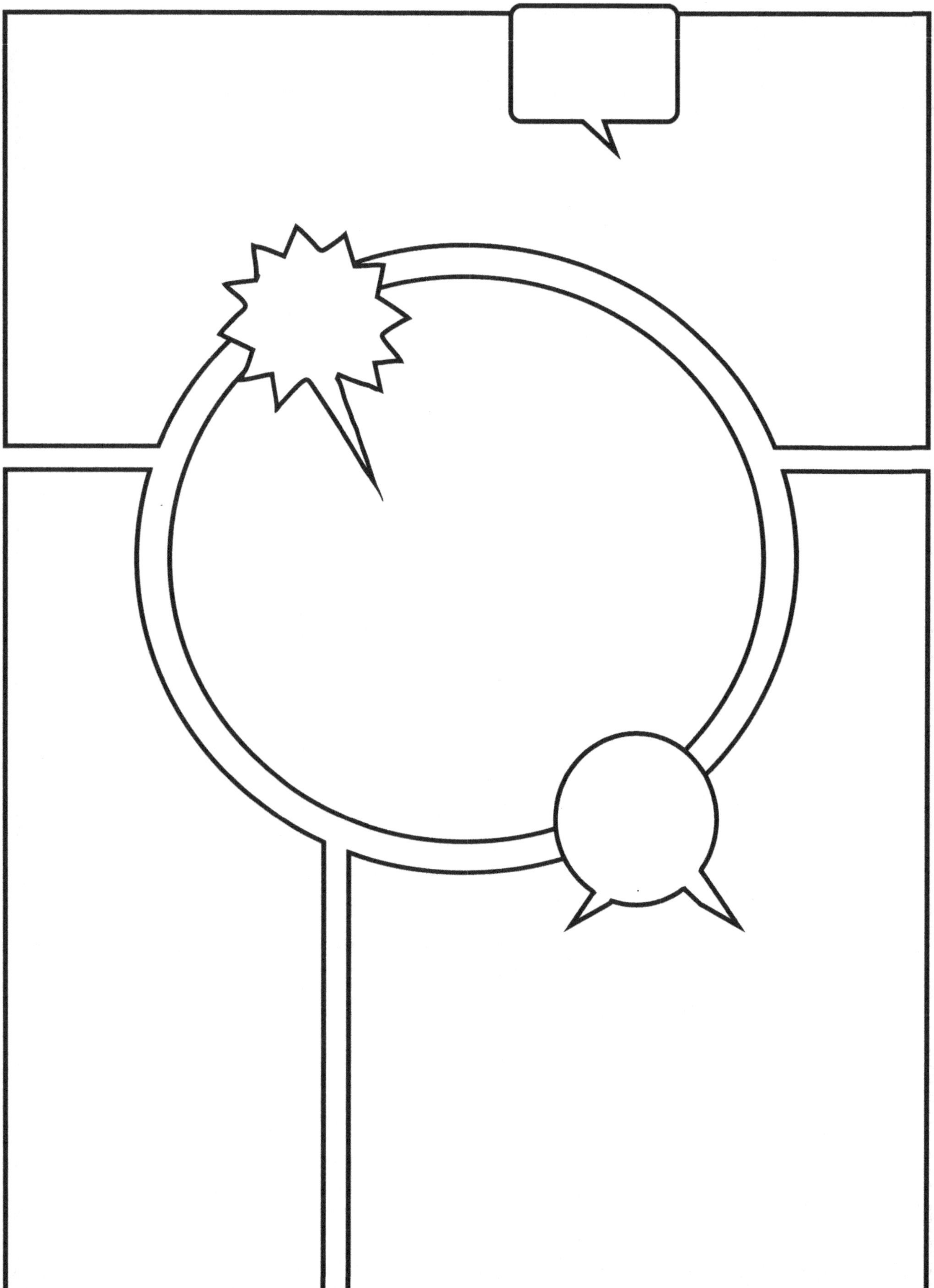

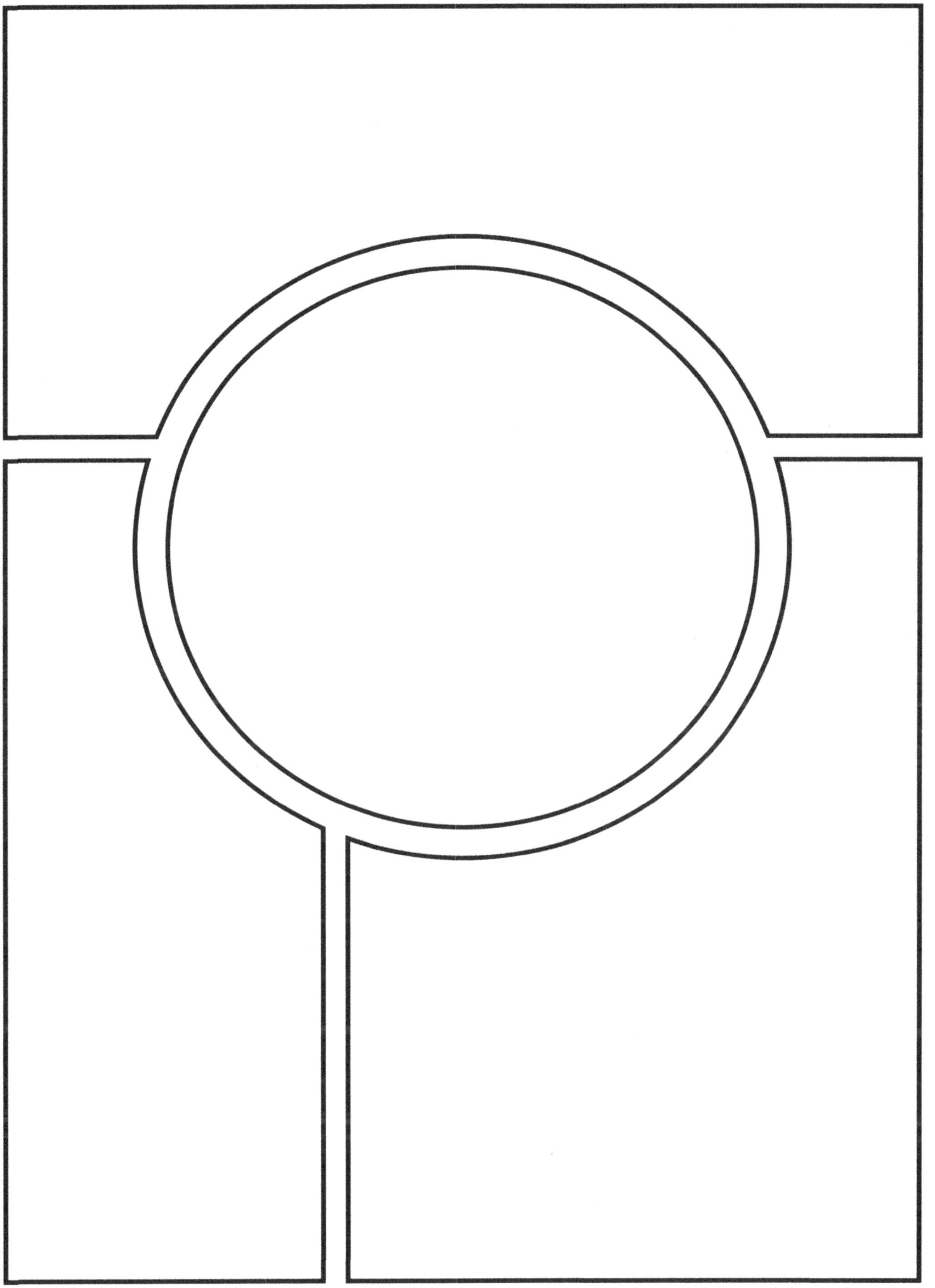

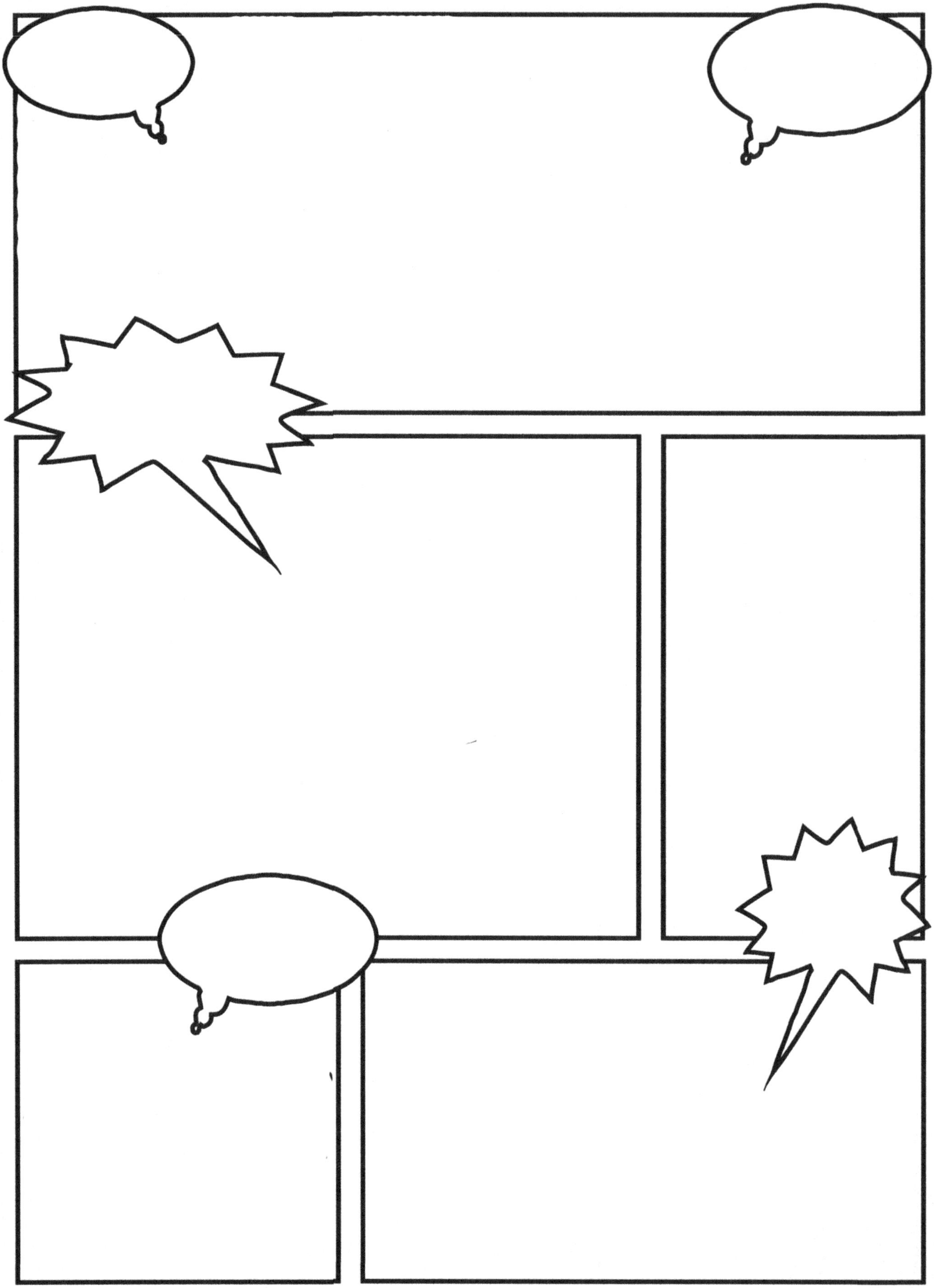

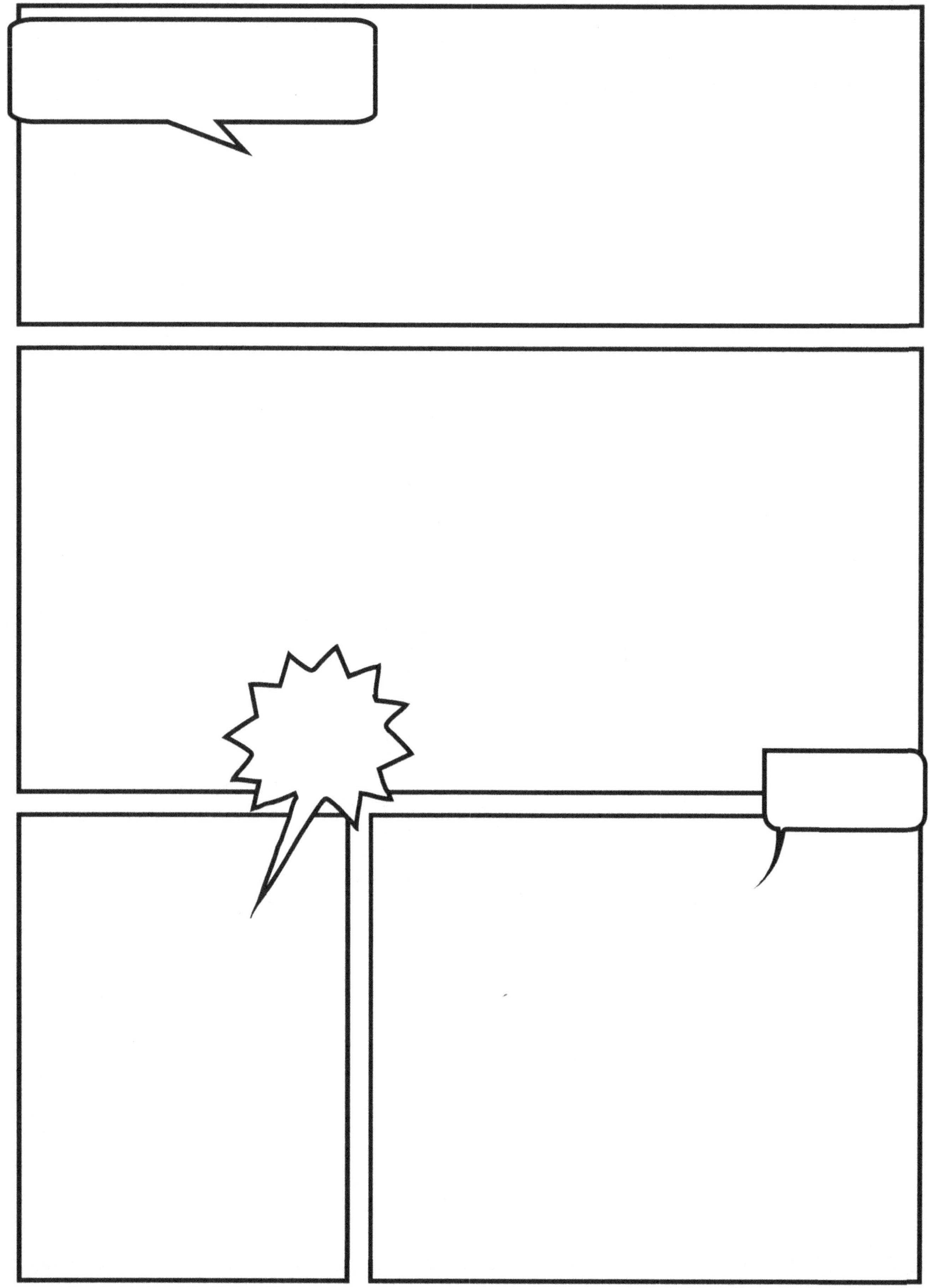

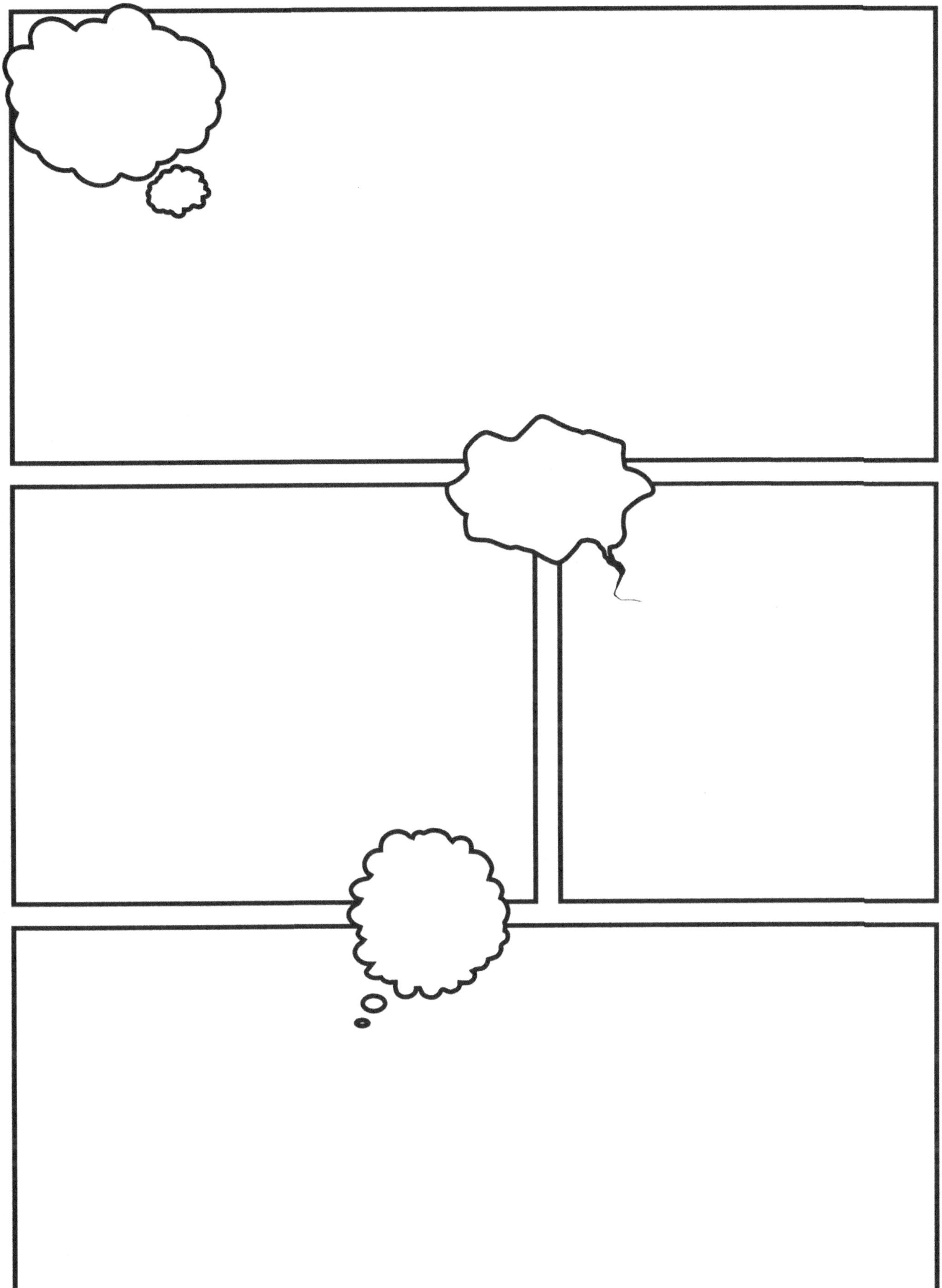

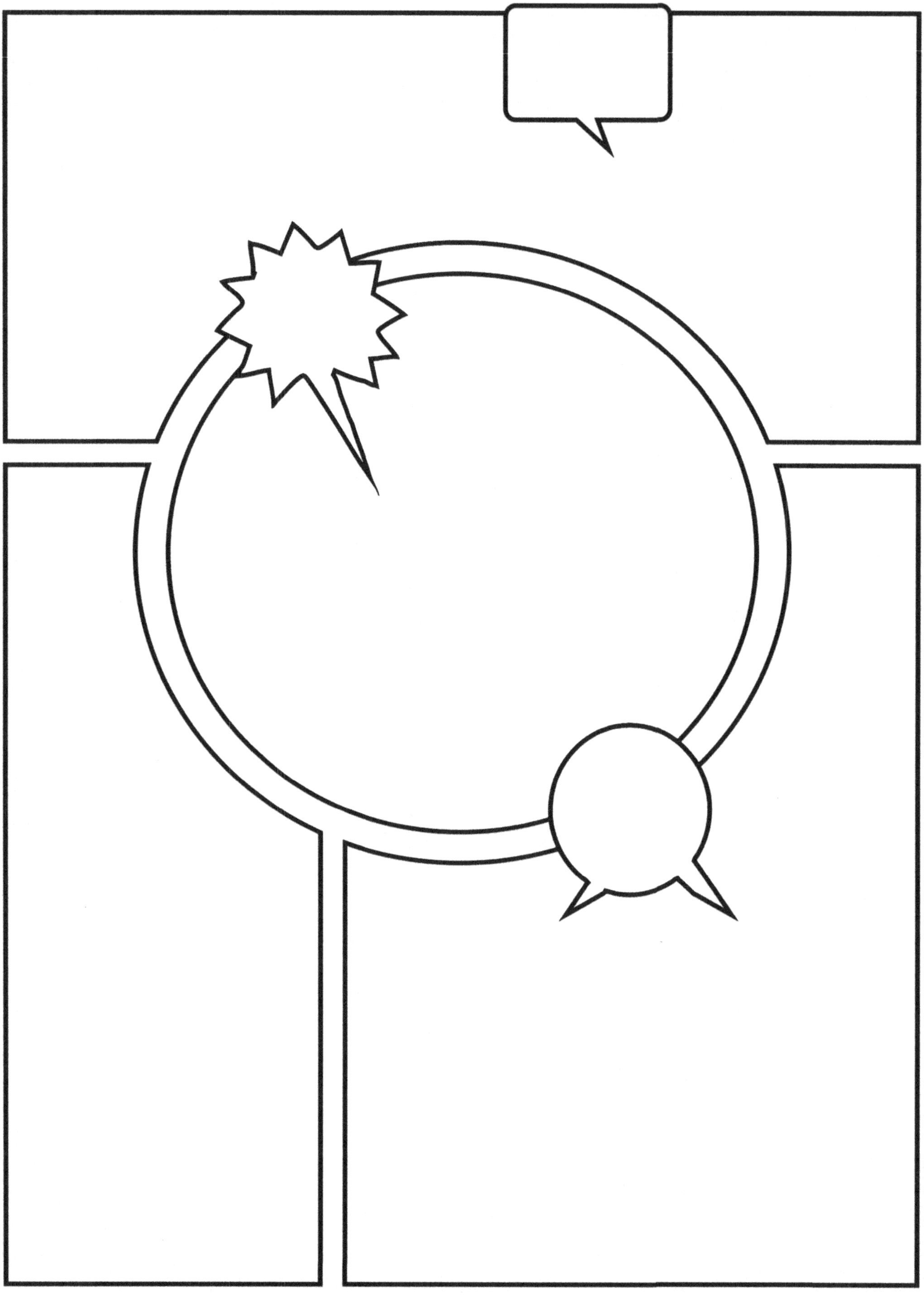

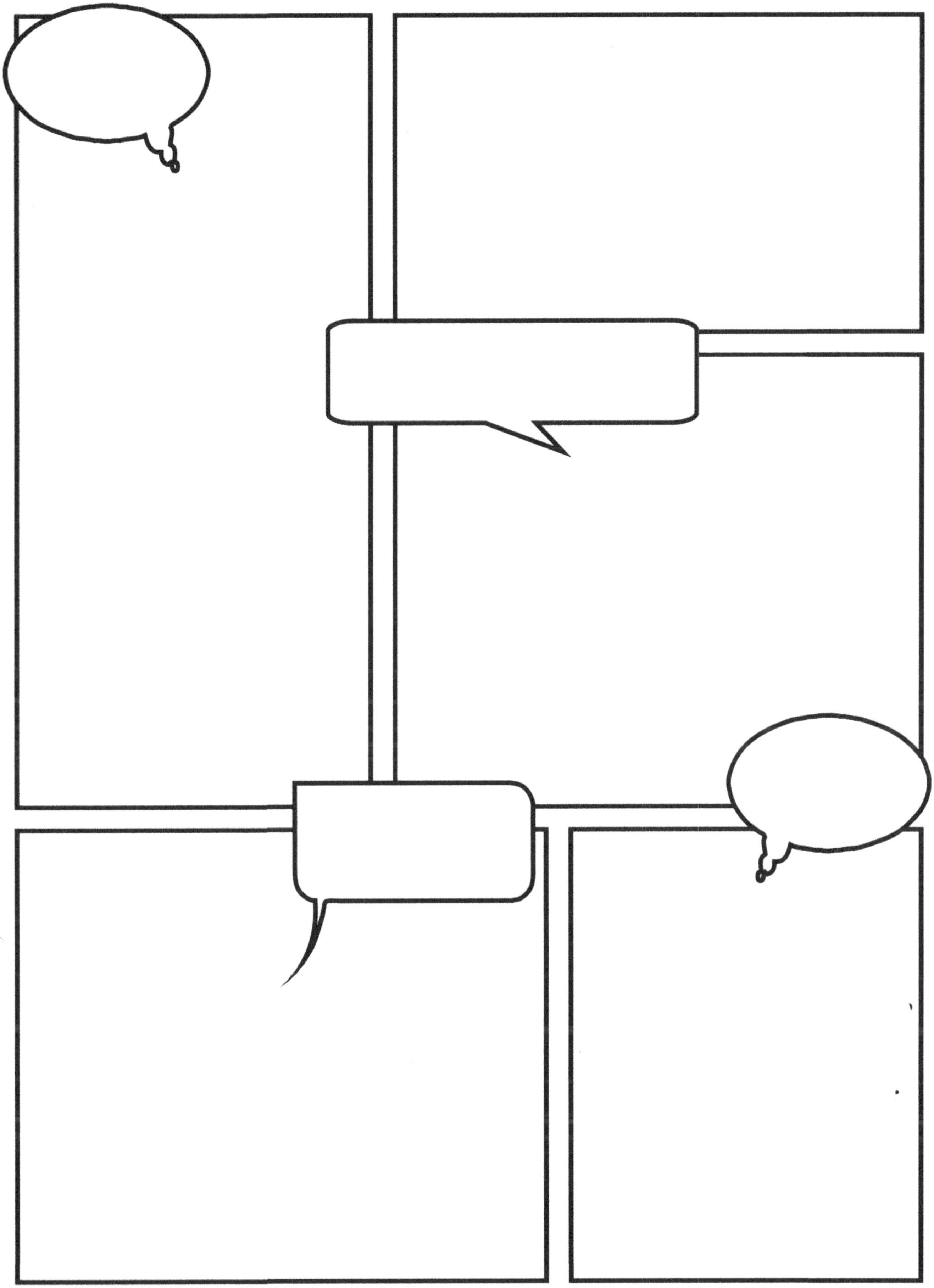

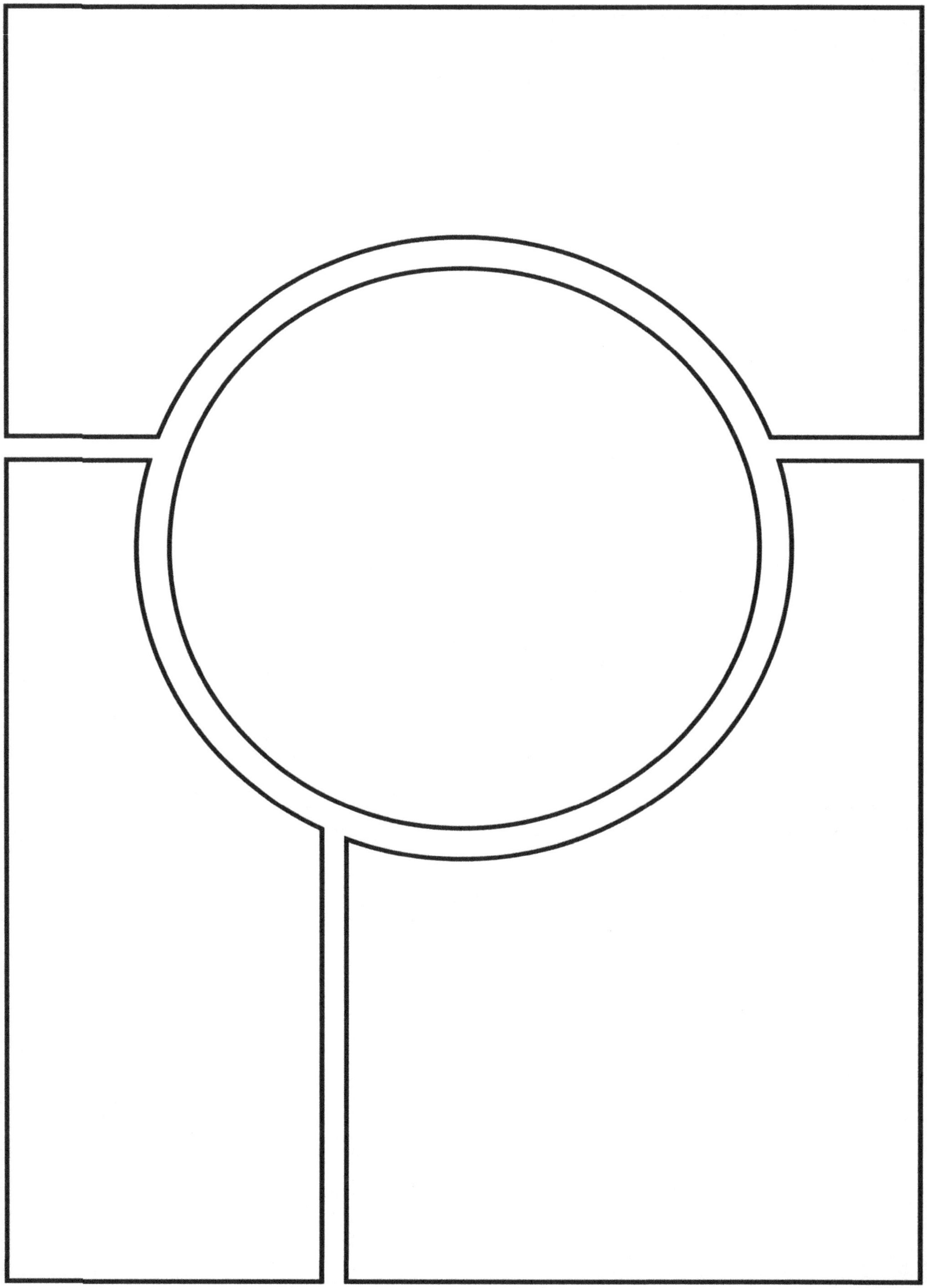

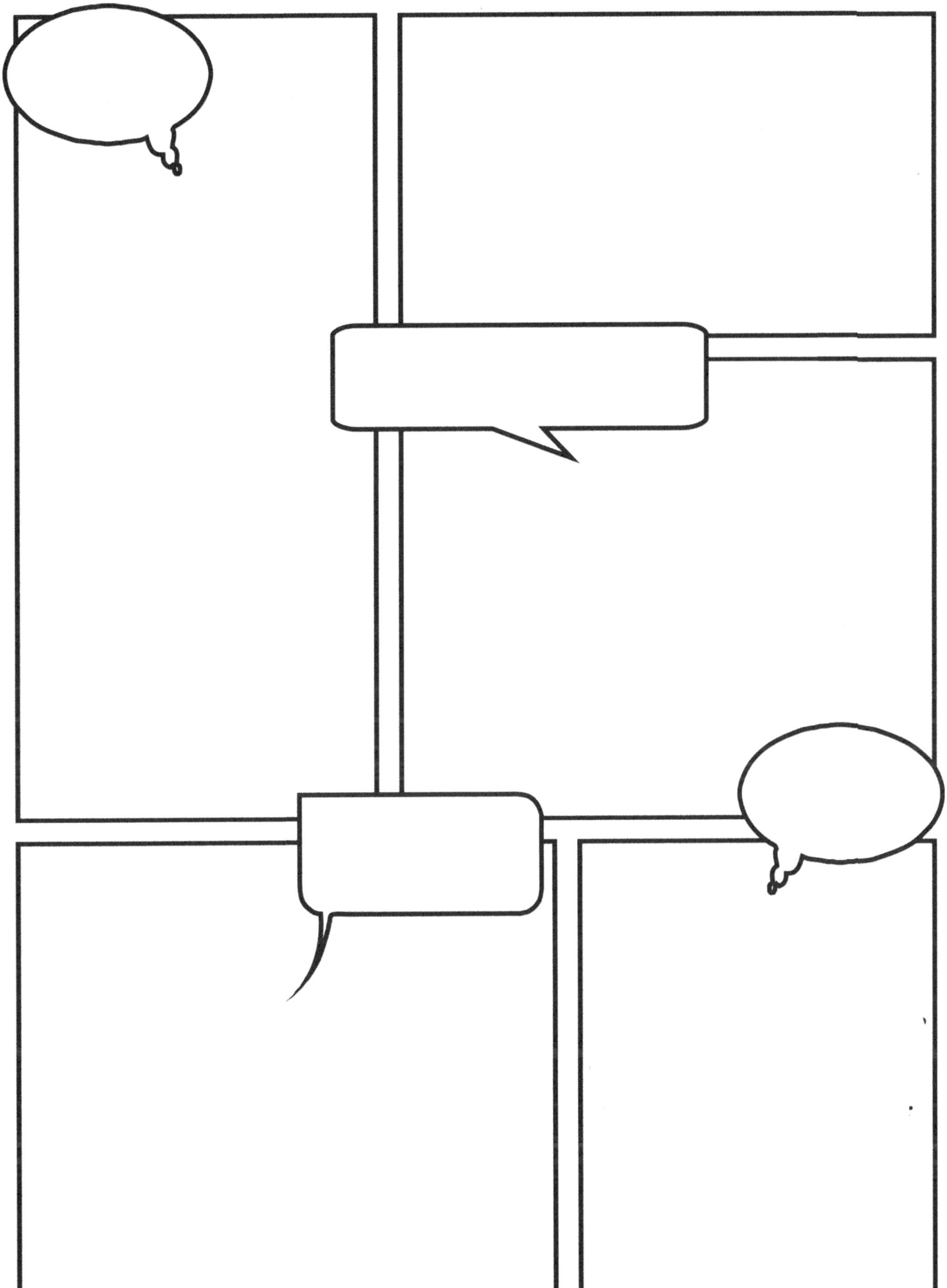

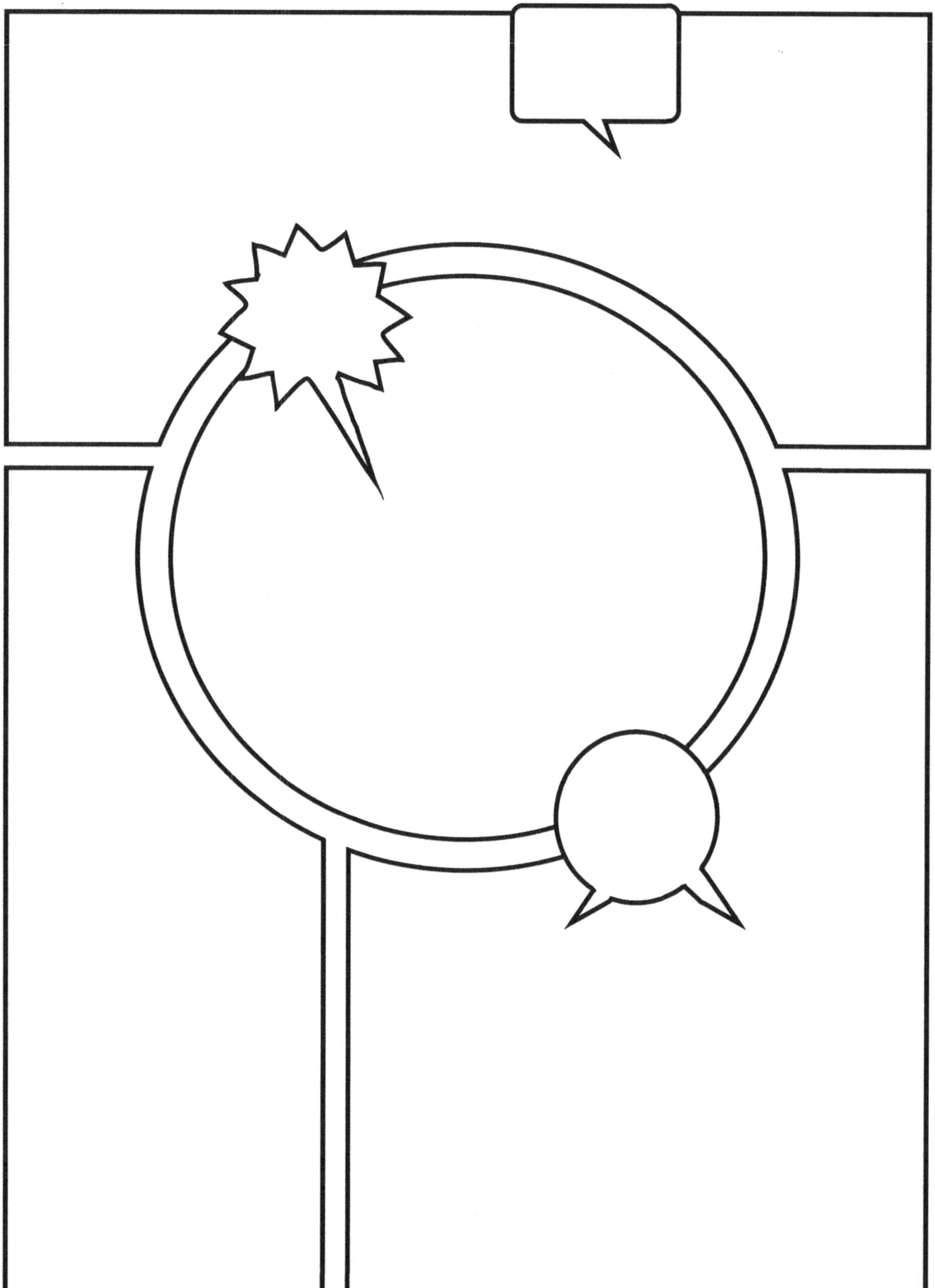

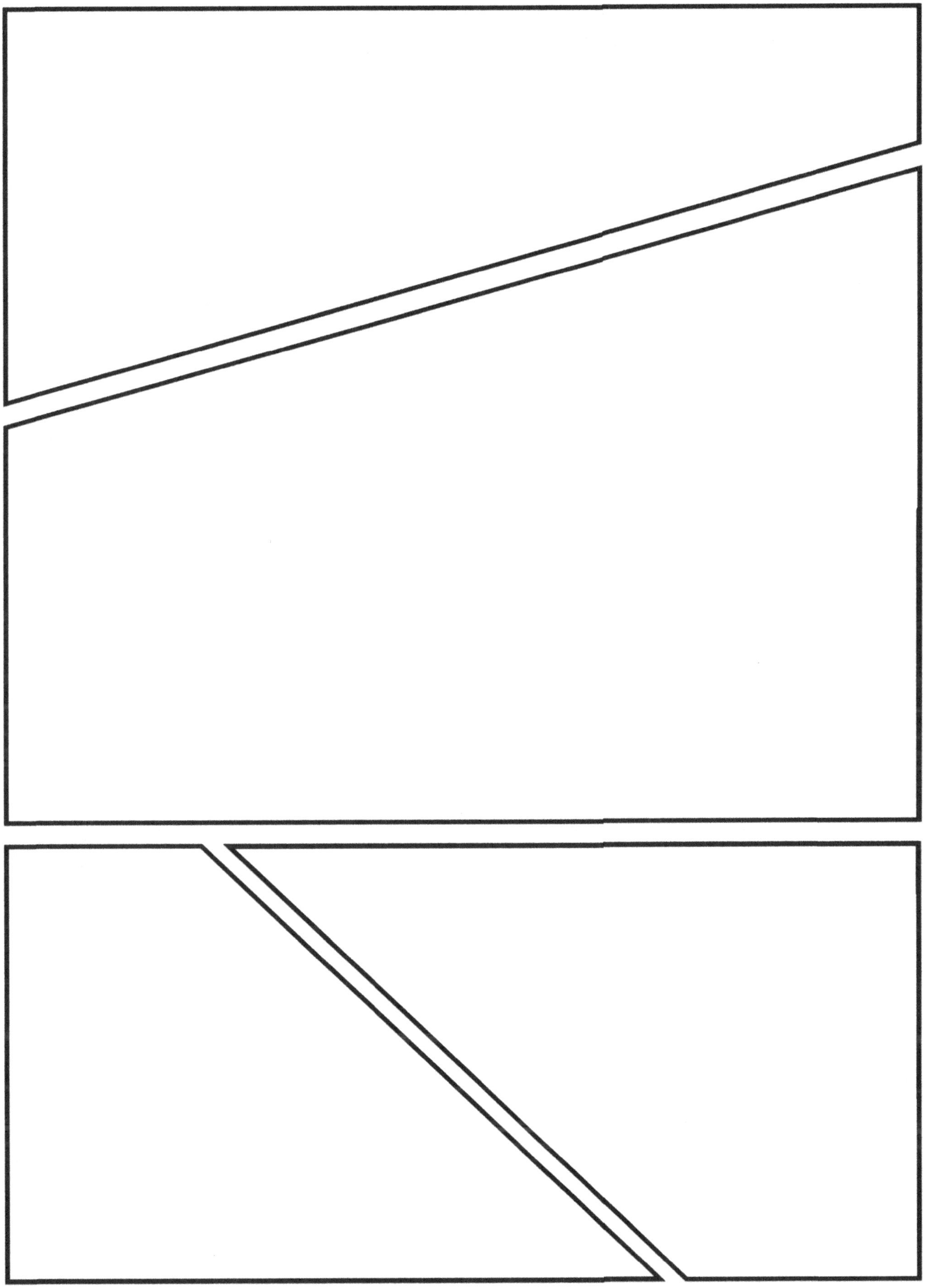

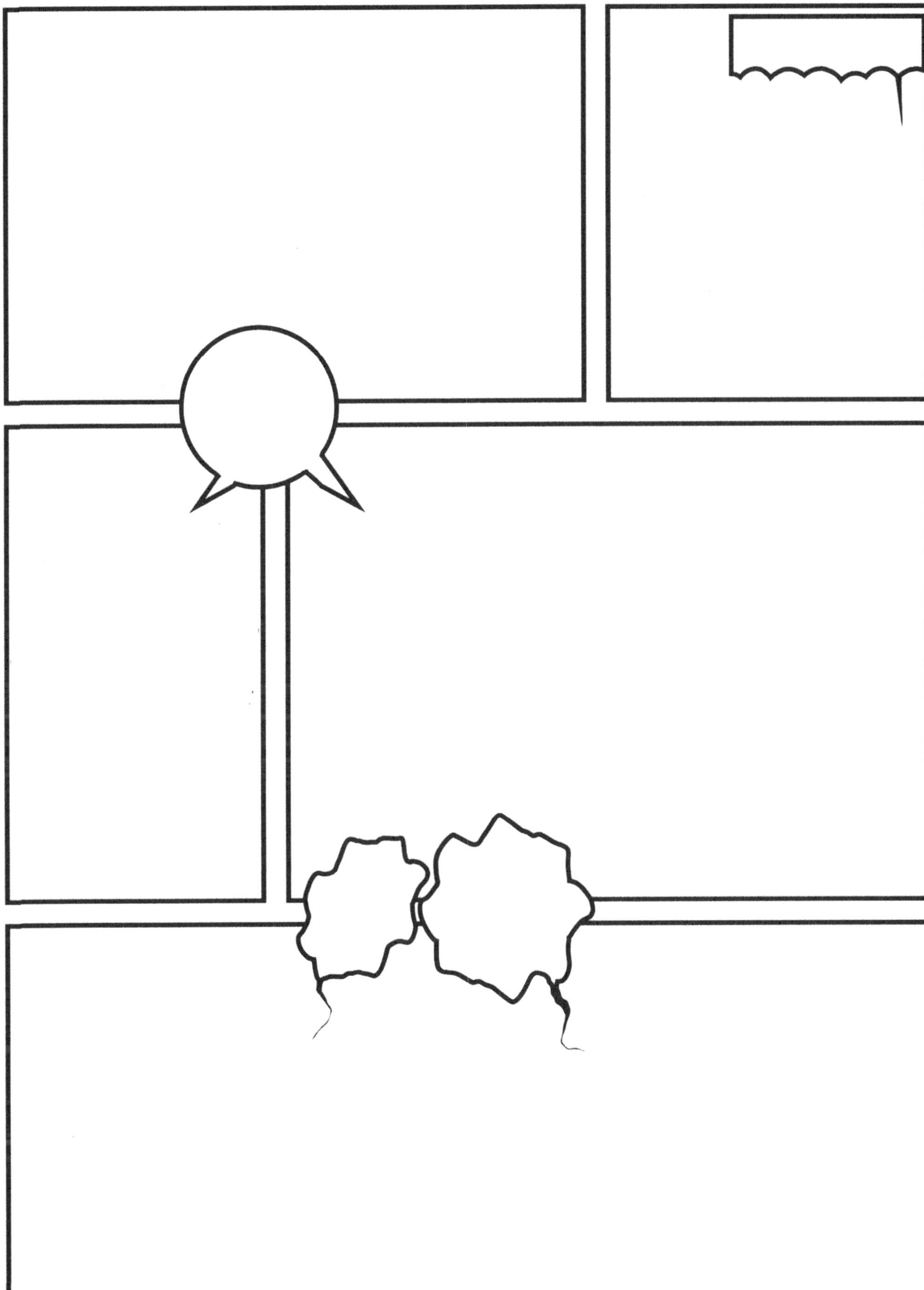

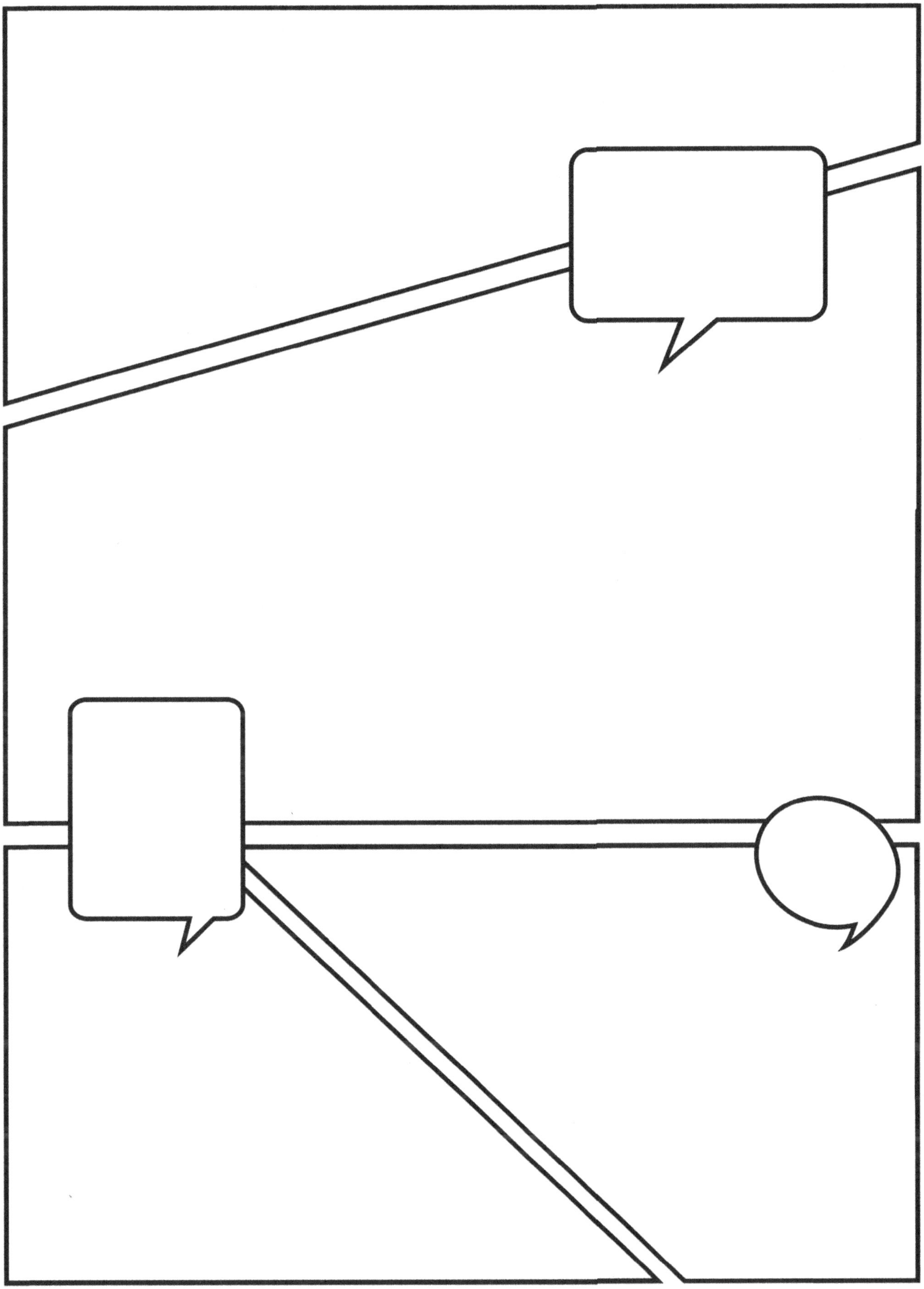

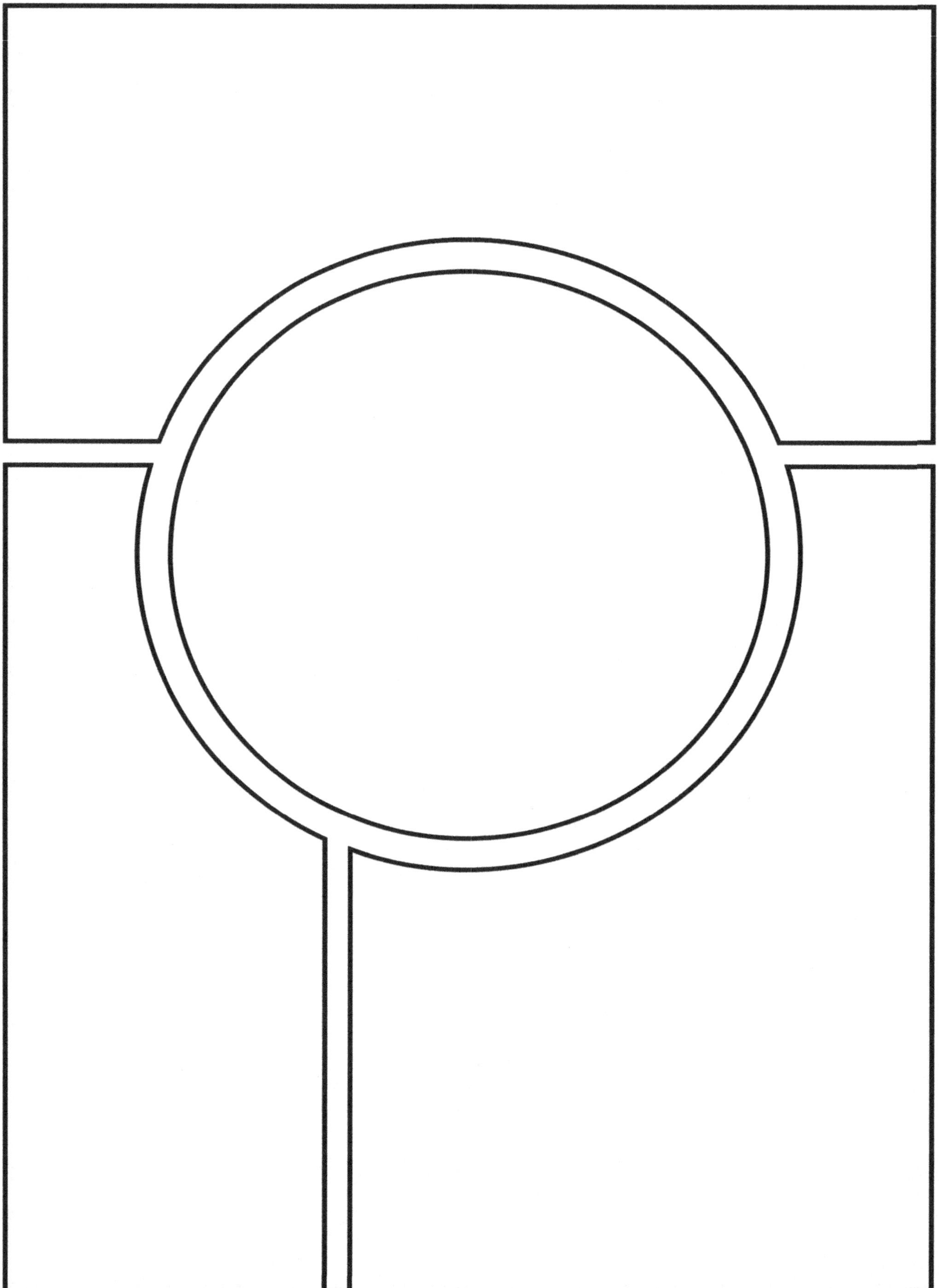

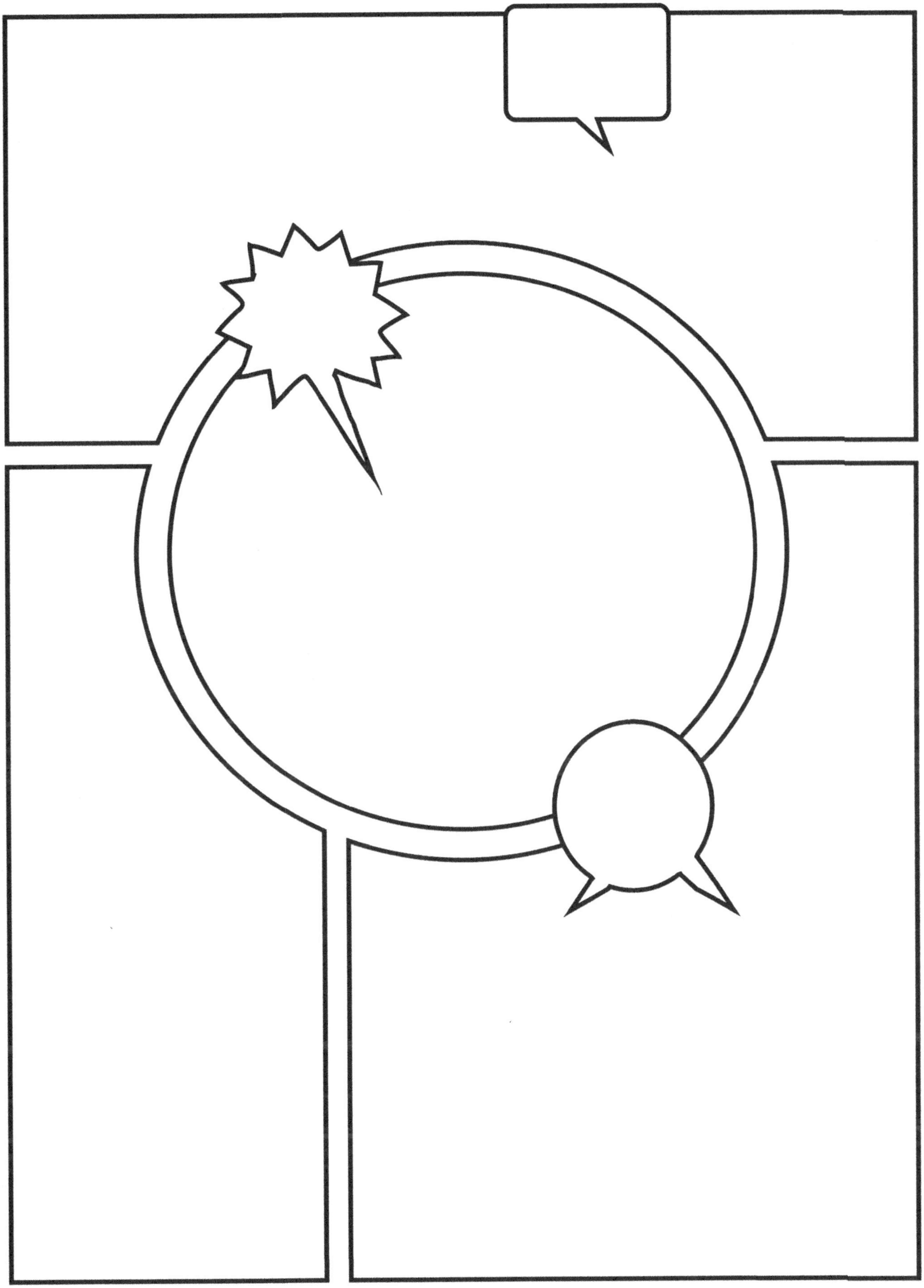

If you need another Blank Comic Book, visit Amazon

If you have enjoyed this book, please consider leaving a review for us so that we can help get this into the hands of more young people.

Thank You

Made in the USA
Middletown, DE
31 October 2021

51366319R00064